THE
DISABLED
GOD

THE
DISABLED
GOD

Toward a Liberatory Theology of Disability

Nancy L. Eiesland

ABINGDON PRESS/Nashville

THE DISABLED GOD:
TOWARD A LIBERATORY THEOLOGY OF DISABILITY

Copyright © 1994 by Abingdon Press

This book is printed on recycled, acid-free paper.

Library of Congress Cataloging-in-Publication Data
Eiesland, Nancy L., 1964–
    The disabled God: toward a liberatory theology of disability/
Nancy L. Eiesland.
        p.   cm.
    Includes bibliographical references and index.
    ISBN 0-687-10801-2 (alk. paper)
    1. Church work with the handicapped.   2. Body. Human—Religious
aspects—Christianity.   3. Theology—Forecasting.   I. Title.
BV4460.E34   1994
261.8'324—dc20
                                                                94-8887
                                                                   CIP

Scripture quotations are taken from the New Revised Standard Version Bible, Copyright 1989 by the Division of Christian Education of the National Council of the Churches of Christ in the USA. Used by permission.

The poem on p. 41 is from REMEMBERING THE BONE HOUSE by NANCY MAIRS. Copyright © 1989 by Nancy Mairs. Reprinted by permission of HarperCollins Publishers, Inc.

Excerpts from CARNAL ACTS by NANCY MAIRS (chap. 2); copyright © 1991 by Nancy Mairs. Reprinted by permission of HarperCollins Publishers, Inc.

98 99 00 01 02 03—10 9 8 7 6 5 4 3

MANUFACTURED IN THE UNITED STATES OF AMERICA

To

UNCLE JAMES *and* AUNT RUTH,

*who taught me by example
that people with disabilities
can live ordinary lives*

CONTENTS

Contents

FOREWORD

Rebecca S. Chopp

N ancy Eiesland's *The Disabled God: Toward a Liberatory Theology of Disability* is a much-needed book for all of us. For persons with disabilities this book creates spaces for "the speaking center," for claiming the realities of ordinary lives. For those, like myself, who are able-bodied this book demands that we examine our practices, our structures, and our images about both persons with disabilities and about able-bodiedness. Most important, this is a much-needed book that moves all of us, persons with disabilities and the able-bodied alike, toward refashioning the social-symbolic order to include liberation for all.

Eiesland identifies her work as a liberation theology. Like other liberation theologies, her work focuses on the voices of persons with disabilities, on oppressive structures and beliefs, and on fashioning new images and practices. Like many liberation theologians, Eiesland derails notions of common human experience and essentialism in Christian symbols. Persons with disabilities define themselves not in some essentialist meaning of disabilities, but rather in a common historical project for liberation. Sharing in and through this project for liberation, persons with disabilities speak of dreams, of desires, of resources, and of struggles in an act of self-naming that is and that anticipates emancipatory transformation.

Eiesland's distinctiveness and power comes, in part, through her care to narrate the interrelated textures of a liberating praxis. First,

9

through the narratives of two women, Diane DeVries and Nancy Mairs, Eiesland portrays the differences in disabilities, in responses to those disabilities, and in the construction of images and beliefs about the body. Second, Eiesland constructs for us a historical narrative of structural responses, both in the oppressive social and symbolic structures that marginalize persons with disabilities, and in legal and social practices, such as the American Disabilities Act of 1990 and the disabilities rights movement, that seek to redress the oppression and belittlement that those with disabilities have suffered. This historical narrative also addresses theoretical models, especially in sociology, that have framed disability in terms of the individual, especially in his or her ability to "adapt." The third narrative texture concerns the ever-present ambiguity in ecclesial reality: romantic beliefs of heroic suffering coupled with structures that force those with disabilities into the margins of ecclesial community. Finally, Eiesland creates new narrative textures that name the possibilities of transformation in the fundamental symbol of the Disabled God and through a new construction of eucharist.

Christian theologians have long maintained the power of symbols to reveal the holy, to constitute community, and to change our beliefs and actions. How symbols function is tied to how they mean in a particular historical context. In what is a rather interesting paradox within Christian symbolic logic, the body is often explicitly denied in importance, and then implicitly constructed through the necessity of only "perfect" bodies representing and approaching God. Indeed, even in the "liberatory" discourse of much feminist theology, a certain romanticization of the body through claims of embodiment inscribes the normal body as the perfect body.

Such an image of the perfect body survives in a network of structures and systems which continually "normalize" the purity of the body. Until the American Disabilities Act of 1990, persons with disabilities (both physical and non-physical) had little recourse to gain equal rights or access. This is symbolized in a most physical way through the construction of even government buildings which only the able-bodied could enter. Acts of charity, especially in the policies of rehabilitation, only strengthen the purity of able-bodiedness as persons with disabilities are "helped" through strategies of

10

paternalistic care to try to adjust like a normal person. Romantic discourses about "overcomers" deny the discriminatory practices and belittling images.

The most astounding fact is, of course, that Christians do not have an able-bodied God as their primal image. Rather, the Disabled God promising grace through a broken body, is at the center of piety, prayer, practice, and mission. Indeed, the centrality of the Disabled God to Christian symbolic logic is a powerful image of resistance to oppressive constructs of "normal embodiment" and an image of transformation for all persons created in the image of God. As Eiesland suggests, the disabling theology of most Christian traditions has equated disabilities with sin. From codes of purity to acts of Jesus' healing, the implicit theological assumption has equated perfect bodies with wholeness of the spirit. And, as if to ensure the quest for purity, physical afflictions become elevated to virtuous suffering when, and only when, they can be spoken of as trials of obedience. Such teachings allow either one of two options for those with disabilities: miraculous healing or heroic suffering.

The image of the Disabled God addresses our imaginations and our practices by weaving together strategies of political action with the re-symbolization of some of our fundamental symbols. Eiesland interprets the Disabled God through a contextualized Christology that speaks of the Incarnation as God with us now. Here the resurrection, the transcendence and perfection of God, reveals true personhood in the ordinariness of life. In this central symbol, full personhood is not presented by the negation, belittlement, or repression of persons with disabilities. Indeed, in spite of the many Christian attempts to deny or negate the literal image itself, the Disabled God represents full personhood as "fully compatible with the experience of disability." In this God, full personhood is lived amidst the ambiguities of life, in the need for care from others, in hope for justice.

Readers, as diverse as we are, will be struck in different ways by the many themes within the texture of the narrative. From my perspective, Eiesland has effected a deep change in conceptions of the body and the natural, or what she calls "natural embodiment." For persons with disabilities ordinary lives are lived in unconven-

11

tional bodies. The tendency to equate disability and tragedy, to romanticize the body and suffering, all must be "unnamed" in Christian theology. These tendencies must be unnamed because persons with disabilities deserve justice, because any and all of us, now or in the future, may have disabilities, and because even the able-bodied person doesn't really fit the image of the "perfect" body that forms our distorted beliefs and practices. In sum, we must change our body practices, including the body practices of how we come to the table, so that the communion becomes not a ritual of exclusion and degradation but a practice of justice, of hope, and of physical presence.

In the first chapter Nancy Eiesland observes that a theological method must work in a kind of back-and-forth fashion. "Persons with disabilities must gain access to the social-symbolic life of the church, and the church must gain access to the social-symbolic lives of people with disabilities." It takes a powerful vision, a mature author, and much passion for justice to accomplish this back-and-forth vision in an area where far too little has been written. Nancy Eiesland has done this, and in so doing invites us to join her in refashioning faith and practice, ecclesia and society, personal beliefs and theoretical models. May we all join her with the grace, clarity, and power that this book models.

Rebecca S. Chopp
Candler School of Theology
Emory University

ACKNOWLEDGMENTS

The bodies we inhabit and the lives those bodies carry on need not be perfect to have value. Bad things do happen, we know—to bad and good people alike—but so do good things. Life's curses, like life's blessings, are always mixed.

Nancy Mairs[1]

Living with a disability is difficult. Acknowledging this difficulty is not a defeat, I have learned, but a hard-won accomplishment in learning to live a life that is not disabled. The difficulty for people with disabilities has two parts really—living our ordinary, but difficult lives, and changing structures, beliefs, and attitudes that prevent us from living ordinarily.

In American society, the temptation to hide our difficulties from others is endemic. For the person with a disability, denial has dangerous consequences. Physically, denial seduces us to ignore glaring physical warning signs. Emotionally, denial leads to atrophy. Ignoring disability means ignoring life; it is the precursor to isolation and powerlessness. Another option for the person with disabilities is to focus on the pain, emotional and physical. For some the pain is great, so it is no wonder that it occupies a prominent place in everyday life. But the telescoping of our lives into simplistic categorizations of good and bad, pain and pleasure, denies that the lives of people with disabilities, like all ordinary lives, are shot through with unexpected grace, overwhelming joy, and love returned. Life is simply a mixed blessing. In this work, I try to chart a middle ground, recognizing in the experience of disability grace

13

and dignity, but not avoiding the disgust and disillusionment of this nonconventional life. If I do not do it perfectly in writing, it is because I do not do it perfectly in life.

As I have written this book I have recalled the many people who taught me to live a difficult life ordinarily. Reared in a North Dakota farming community, I learned a good deal about ordinary life and incarnate love. My parents, Dean and Carol Arnold, contended with pendulous grain prices, the vagaries of the weather, and Blue Cross and Blue Shield to ensure that I got the care I needed. Their love and support, together with that of my brothers, Neal and Victor, and my sisters, Kathleen Arnold, Suzanne Chole (deceased), and Jocelyn Gracza, have emboldened and strengthened me.

I am also deeply indebted to a long line of talented and committed educators. With the enactment of the Education for All Handicapped Children Act of 1975, requiring public school systems to provide free and appropriate public education, I was enrolled in a small-town grade school where what was now the law regarding educating children with disabilities had already always been the moral obligation of these teachers. I am especially grateful to my high school creative writing teacher, Barbara Johnson, who responded to my disgust that I had nothing to write about because I had just spent the last months in the hospital, for encouraging me to write about my "ordinary life." Beginning during many long hospital stays in my childhood, I long cherished the mistaken notion that books were for escape. Through the years, educators have changed my mind. Books should inspire action; good books may even help us live better lives, individually and collectively. Dr. Rebecca S. Chopp's work, in particular, has empowered me to think and act.

My friends and colleagues during my doctoral work at Emory University—Emily Brooker-Langston, Mary Ann Zimmer, Barbara Elwell, David Ahearn, Bobbi Patterson, Janet Jakobsen, Ken Brooker-Langston, Carolyn Olson, Scott Thumma, Laurel Kearns, Steve Olson, and Mary Davidson—have listened to ideas, read portions of the text, and provided encouragement throughout this project. Dr. Pam Couture, who directed this work as my Master's thesis at Candler School of Theology, has given me support, comments, corrections, and ideas. Dr. Nancy Ammerman has taught by example how one could combine sociological analysis and commitment to people of faith. My editor, Ulrike Guthrie, has been a spirited supporter and friend. Terry Eiesland, my husband, has taught me the strength of interdependence. Without his advocacy, energy, and love, I would not be the person I am, nor this work what it is. Finally, this book grows out of a commitment to acknowledge and appreciate the many people with disabilities who have worked for the simple right to work, to get on a bus, and to be seen for who they are instead of what they aren't. These are the people who have energized me.

Although many people have contributed to this work, its shortcomings are solely my responsibility. The trouble with making a start is that it is always only a start, never the final word. This book is a beginning—an invitation to further work by people with disabilities and a call to all "others who care" to engage people with disabilities as historical actors and theological subjects. In the end, this work will be incomplete because the lives and body of people with disabilities continue to evolve.

THE DISABLED GOD

CHAPTER ONE

COMING TO TERMS

The Nation's proper goals regarding individuals with disabilities are to assure equality of opportunity, full participation, independent living, and economic self-sufficiency.

Americans with Disabilities Act of 1990

People with disabilities finally have our own emancipation proclamation. For the 43 million Americans (approximately one in every six) who are disabled, the Americans with Disabilities Act (ADA) of 1990 is landmark legislation declaring equality for people with disabilities. The ADA, patterned after the Civil Rights Act of 1964, challenges myths, attitudes, segregationist practices, and working conditions that have kept many people with disabilities in poverty and housebound. This civil rights legislation equates denying people with disabilities access to employment, buildings, public accommodations, transportation, or communication services with denying access to someone on the basis of race, religion, or gender. The legislation's passage capped a decade of unparalleled social change benefiting the disabled.

The spirit of liberation and opportunity evidenced in ADA was catalyzed by the concerted efforts of the modern disability rights movement. Following the racial, gender, and other civil rights movements in the 1960s, this diverse group of people with disabilities engaged in political activism and action, demanding integration into the American mainstream. Emboldened by collective power, people with disabilities began to break through the social stigmatization and marginalization that had rendered us silent and invisible, pursuing our right to full civic and economic participation and the removal of social and physical barriers.

The liberatory impulse evidenced in the disability rights movement has propelled people with disabilities to resist their marginal status in the full range of social institutions, including the Christian church. Calling for the church to take a leading role in promoting our full humanity, people with disabilities have protested restrictive ordination requirements. We have resisted our experience being reformulated to conform to crippling theological categories. We have recovered our hidden history and exposed the church's complicity with our marginality.

The history of the church's interaction with the disabled is at best an ambiguous one. Rather than being a structure for empowerment, the church has more often supported the societal structures and attitudes that have treated people with disabilities as objects of pity and paternalism. For many disabled persons the church has been a "city on a hill"—physically inaccessible and socially inhospitable.

Today most denominations and many local congregations realize that church facilities should be constructed or altered to encourage the presence of persons with disabilities. Yet little effort has been made to promote the full participation of people with disabilities in the life of the church. The emergent experiences of people with disabilities as historical actors and theological subjects have wide-ranging implications for theological interpretations of central Christian beliefs and practices.

ACCESSIBLE THEOLOGICAL METHOD

In relation to a theology of disability, the measure of the usefulness of a practical theological method is accessibility. A theological method must provide two-way access. Persons with disabilities must gain access to the social-symbolic life of the church, and the church must gain access to the social-symbolic lives of people with disabilities. In such access two agendas must be recognized. The first and primary agenda is enabling people with disabilities to participate fully in the life of the church. Rebecca S. Chopp's critical praxis correlation furthers this end. Critiquing David Tracy's revised critical correlation method, Chopp highlights two distortions therein: the tendency toward a universalized "common human experience" and an underlying assumption of the at-home-ness within Christian tradition.[1] She asserts that Tracy's notion of the "common human experience" tends to rationalize and homogenize the variety of human experience to arrive at something approximating social consensus. She argues instead for a theological method that encompasses difference, specificity, embodiment, solidarity, anticipation, and transformation.[2] Further in her criticism of Tracy's basic at-home-ness within Christian tradition, she appeals not for the rejection of the Christian tradition, but for a full recognition that not all people have enjoyed this comfortable relationship with the church, primarily because the church has refused to address them in ways that affirm their dignity and self-understanding. These two insights are vital in assessing the accessibility of any theological method. Clearly a method that fails to question the "common human experience" would continue to isolate people with disabilities while purporting to include them. Furthermore, the experience of people with disabilities within the church has never been one of "at-home-ness," as just noted.

David Tracy responds to Chopp's criticism by agreeing that individual persons and communities are the primary locus for theological thought. He further argues that his position does consider a broad range of correlations with the Christian tradition. Tracy restates his position as the following:

There is nothing in the "revised correlational model" that demands a "liberal" solution. There is only the demand—the properly theological demand—that whatever and whoever the practical theologian is, she or he is bound by the very nature of the enterprise as theological to show how one interprets the tradition and how one interprets the present situation and how those two interpretations correlate: as either identities of meaning, analogies, or radical nonidentities.[3]

21

Chopp's critical praxis correlation engages a strategy that works its way forward through the interplay between what is already known to the theologian and active engagement with the particular people who teach them to rework their theories, labels, and depictions of reality. Chopp identifies the aim of critical praxis correlation as emancipatory transformation of the social-symbolic order, which includes the dominant practices and principles of language, subjectivity, and politics. Moments in the method include a de-ideologization of scriptures, a pragmatic interpretation of experience, a critical theory of emancipation and enlightenment, and a social theory to transform praxis.[4] This liberatory theology of disability includes a deliberate recognition of the lived experience of persons with disability, a critical analysis of a social theory of disability and of certain aspects of the church's institutional practices and Christian theology, and the proclamation of emancipatory transformation.

Chopp invokes corporeality or embodiment in her formulation of emancipatory transformation, laying the groundwork for identifying the body as a locus for theological reflection. Unless the notion of embodiment is deliberately deconstructed, the cultural norms of "body as natural" seep into the subtext. In my use of the theological method outlined by Chopp, I concentrate on the "mixed blessing" of the body in the real, lived experience of people with disabilities and explicitly deconstruct any norms which are part of the unexpressed agenda of "normal embodiment." My own body composed as it is of metal and plastic, as well as bone and flesh, is my starting point for talking about "bones and braces bodies" as a norm of embodiment.

The body is crucial to both the micro and macro orders of society. Social theorist Bryan S. Turner writes: "The body is the vehicle for self-performances and the target through rituals of degradation of social exclusion."[5] Thus deliberate attention to the physical body is necessary in order to prevent it from becoming socially erased or subsumed into notions of normal embodiment. An accessible theological method necessitates that the body be represented as flesh and blood, bones and braces, and not simply the rationalized realm of activity.

22

The second agenda in two-way access is discovering a means by which the church can gain access to the social-symbolic life of persons with disabilities. Here I employ Paul Ricoeur's phenomenology of symbolism. Two-way access necessitates that the Christian tradition recognize the lived experience of persons with disabilities and that people with disabilities are able to acknowledge the symbols of the Christian tradition, not as over against us, but as a part of our hidden history. Ricoeur asserts that between rejection and uncritical acceptance of symbols and myths there is a third model, which he indicates with the aphorism, "The symbol gives rise to thought."[6] He asserts that meditation on symbols "starts from speech that has already taken place and in which everything has already been said in some fashion."[7] The task of his phenomenology then is not to telescope history into a generic universal symbol, but to remember what has been symbolized already and how complex those symbols are. The phenomenological approach properly used is bound to temporality and can bridge to physicality.

In this project, the historical moment of remembrance is embodied in Jesus Christ, the disabled God, present in resurrection and in the church and broken anew at each eucharistic reenactment. The symbol of Jesus Christ, the disabled God, is both gift and enigma, enabling a two-way access through his broken body. The dissonance raised by the nonacceptance of persons with disabilities and the acceptance of grace through Christ's broken body necessitates that the church find new ways of interpreting disability. This work identifies the narratives of people with disabilities themselves as the place to begin. These accounts tell us about the ordinary lives of people with nonconventional bodies.

THE SOCIAL CONSTRUCTION OF DISABILITY

Exactly who "people with disabilities" are is not, however, self-evident. The differences among persons with disabilities are often so profound that few areas of commonality exist. People with disabilities have a wide variety of physical, psychological, and intel-

23

lectual impairments. Different conditions produce different types of functional impairment. For instance, deafness, paralysis, multiple sclerosis, and mental retardation may produce the same social problems of stigma, marginality, and discrimination, but they generate vastly different functional difficulties. Further, people with the same disability may differ significantly in the extent of their impairment. The level of impairment for a person with dyslexia may be dramatically dissimilar to that of a person with severe mental retardation, though they can both be identified as having learning disabilities. Finally, disabilities can be either static or progressive, congenital or acquired. The social experience of a person who becomes disabled as an adult may differ significantly from that of a person with a congenital disability. These dissimilarities make a broad definition of people with disabilities difficult, if not impossible.

However, people with disabilities are distinguished not because of our shared physical, psychological, or emotional traits, but because "temporarily able-bodied" persons single us out for differential treatment.[8] Although people with disabilities span a broad spectrum of medical conditions with diverse effects on appearance and function, studies indicate that whatever the setting, whether in education, medicine, rehabilitation, social welfare policy, or society at large, a common set of stigmatizing values and arrangements has historically operated against us.[9] This recognition has led activists and sociologists to argue that persons with disabilities constitute a minority group, shaped primarily by exclusion.[10]

In this work, the minority group model will be used to identify the social situation of people with disabilities. In using this I make not only a sociological argument, but also a political statement of solidarity with the disability rights movement. As a person with disability involved with the disability rights movement, I use sociological theories and methods that empower and provide a foundation for political action. I will explore more completely the sociological implications of this minority group framework in chapter 3.

Chapter 2 is a retelling of the experiences and emergent self-understandings of two women with disabilities, Nancy Mairs and

24

Diane DeVries. These women confound stereotypic conceptions of the lives of people with disabilities, revealing themselves instead as historical actors and theological subjects. Chapter 3 offers a social framework for reconceiving disability, incorporating the history of the civil rights struggle and the minority group model of disability. In chapter 4, I identify theological themes that handicap people with disabilities and present a historical case study from the American Lutheran Church revealing the institutional praxes of segregation and discrimination against us. For people with disabilities, full inclusion within the community of God calls for new symbols, practices, and beliefs. Together people with disabilities and the able-bodied must be reconciled with the disabled God through Jesus Christ's broken body in eucharistic repentance and celebration. In chapter 5, I recover the hidden history of the disabled God and propose a paradigm for wholeness, power, and perfection—a liberatory theology of disability. In chapter 6, I discuss the eucharistic celebration of this disabled God and the reformulation of the Eucharist as a ritual enactment of inclusion for people with disabilities.

COMING TO TERMS

As linguists and anthropologists know, the act of naming someone or something grants the namer power over the named. Historically, rather than naming ourselves, the disabled have been named by medical and scientific professionals or by people who denied our full personhood. These professionals considered disabled persons to be less intelligent, less capable of making the "right" decisions, less "realistic," less logical, and less self-directed than non-disabled persons. Thus "capable" persons and experts needed to define the experience of disabled individuals. Therefore, there has been a scarcity of substantial, direct information concerning the feelings, goals, and self-definitions of disabled persons.[11] However, alongside the changes in legislation and public attitudes brought about by the disability rights movement have come changes in the language used to describe disability and changes in who does the describing. Persons with disabilities have become the subjects of our own lives, identifying our own needs and ambitions, and naming ourselves. People with disabilities today use language that highlights our own self-understanding as people with full and "normal" lives, rather than the social stereotypes, which emphasize passivity and dependence. So naming the experience of disability is no mere exercise in semantics or a matter of personal preference, it is part of the political work of empowerment.

Two questions are germane to our efforts to come to terms: which name shall be employed with regularity? and in what context shall the term be understood? Some of the possible options include "crippled," "handicapped," "disabled," "physically challenged," "person with disability," and more. While in this book I use "persons with disabilities," other terms have been utilized by various individuals and groups. Expressions such as "cripple" and "gimp" have generally gone out of favor within the disabled community because of their negative connotations of passivity and the implication that impairment is the primary identifiable attribute. Nonetheless, some people with disabilities continue to use "cripple" as a rhetorical device. Nancy Mairs, a well-known essayist and person with multiple sclerosis, employs the term "cripple" for herself. She uses the word because of its starkness and precision and rejects "disabled" because of its ambiguous referent, which may express any incapacity, physical or intellectual. Likewise, she refuses "handicapped" because it implies an active agent who accomplished the handicapping.[12] Although Mairs uses "cripple" as self-descriptive, she writes, "I would never refer to another person as a cripple. It is the word I use to name only myself."[13] Although "cripple" may be reinterpreted to be personally empowering, the social construction of the term and its continuing derogatory usage make it generally unacceptable to persons with disabilities.

Euphemisms for persons with disabilities have abounded in recent years, including "differently abled," "physically challenged," and "handicapable." Different terms have gained varying degrees of acceptance among persons with disabilities. Some persons reject these terms as verbal garbage, arguing that they describe everyone and no one. These people maintain that euphemisms deny the fact that disabilities really do exist and reinforce the idea that disabilities must be camouflaged to make them acceptable for public discourse. Other disabled individuals have found some terms, particularly "physically challenged," to be useful and appropriate to their experience.

In the debate over the language of disability, people with disabilities are rejecting the stigmatized social identity imposed upon us and are identifying themselves.[14] Although different individuals may designate themselves with various terms, the current phrase acceptable to most persons with disabilities is just that, "persons with disabilities." This usage underscores the conviction that an individual's disability is just one of many personal characteristics, rather than being synonymous or coextensive with that person's self. In recent civil rights legislation, including the Americans with Disabilities Act of 1990, the expression "persons with disabilities" is employed most regularly. In the literature of the disability rights movement, this designation is also the predominant one.

Important distinctions drawn between terms such as "impairment," "disability," and "handicap" are significant for this work.[15] "Impairment" refers to an abnormality or loss of physiological form or function. "Disability" describes the consequences of the impairment, that is an inability to perform some task or activity considered necessary. This corresponds with the most generally accepted definition of disability as "a form of inability or limitation in performing roles or tasks expected of an individual within a social environment."[16] "Handicap," on the other hand, generally denotes a social disadvantage that results from an impairment or disability.[17] Thus an impairment does not necessarily result in a disability, and a disability need not be a handicap, so defined. While these distinctions are customarily used by professionals, they occupy the middle ground between popular and technical language.

In this work, the designation "persons with disabilities" will refer to persons with physical disabilities only, except when otherwise noted. To be sure, it would be a worthwhile and much-needed project to examine the experience of persons with intellectual, social, or emotional disabilities within the church. However, such endeavors are outside the scope of this work. One reason for

27

excluding these important concerns is the prominence of physical disability in the sociological theory and the theological argument employed here. Second, although the stigmatization of persons with intellectual, social, and emotional disabilities is largely similar to that of persons with physical disabilities, the phenomena also differ in important ways. Identifying and exploring these differences also is outside the scope of this work. Nonetheless, the paucity of theological exploration of social, emotional, and intellectual disabilities is scandalous. It is my hope that this book will encourage others to ask and explore theological questions concerning a broad spectrum of disability.

"Access" or "accessibility" has become a rallying cry among people with disabilities. I use it here as both a rhetorical and a technical term. It is not restricted to physical modifications in personal living space or limited facilities. Rather it is understood as participation, as well as mobility, throughout society as a legally protected right.[18] People with disabilities have been encouraged to see our needs as unique and extraordinary, rather than as society-wide issues of inclusion and exclusion. Accessibility then means the availability of the same choices accorded to able-bodied people. It also means opening the meaning of "normal" to the ordinary lives of people with disabilities. Accessibility as used here refers to social-symbolic, physical, and legal inclusion in the common life.

I have chosen women as witnesses in chapter 2. Although I do not suggest that the experience of white women can stand as representative for all people with disabilities, I do maintain that their experiences are relevant to all people with disabilities and all able-bodied people. They are witnesses not to the full diversity of people with disabilities but rather to the new systems of valuation and practices of subversion that many people with disabilities embody as constitutive of our ordinary lives. However, I am aware of the danger of the "false universalism" of feminist writing in the 1970s and have noted the tendency within disability rights literature to stress commonalities among all people with disabilities rather than differences based on gender, race, ethnicity, sexual orientation, or social class. This tendency is partly due to the lack of research and the paucity of autobiographical accounts of the varied experiences among people with disabilities. In this work, I am making a strategic judgment to emphasize in the experiences of women with disabilities ordinary themes that are meaningful for many people with disabilities. This judgment does not mean, however, that I am unaware or uninterested in the differences among people with disabilities. It simply underscores the interdependence of our fate as persons with disabilities and makes possible an understanding of our existence as a disadvantaged minority group. For people with disabilities, coalitions of groups and individuals with diverse impairments have always been the norm. Within these coalitions we have had to work hard, and not always successfully, to identify the ways issues of gender, race, ethnicity, sexual orientation, and class interact with our experiences of disability. My contention is that a liberatory theology of disability is a theology of coalition and struggle in which we identify our unique experiences while also struggling for recognition, inclusion, and acceptance from one another and from the able-bodied society and church.

CHAPTER TWO

BODIES OF KNOWLEDGE

The place which my body occupies within the world, my actual Here is the starting point from which I take my bearings in space. It is, so to speak, the center 0 in my system of coordinates.

Alfred Schutz[1]

The corporeal is for people with disabilities the most real. Unwilling and unable to take our bodies for granted, we attend to the kinesis of knowledge.[2] That is, we become keenly aware that our physical selves determine our perceptions of the social and physical world. These perceptions, like our bodies, are often nonconforming and disclose new categories and models of thinking and being.

These new embodied categories arise from the concrete experiences of people with disabilities. For this reason, the specific stories of people with disabilities are prerequisites for a liberatory theology of disability. Yet our stories have often been misused. Our distinct narratives have too frequently been simplistically recast into standard tales of "overcomers," a genre of disability literature that elevates the individual who conquers disability and achieves success. These stories often leave the impression that with great personal effort people with disabilities can overcome our physical limitations and the social barriers. They emphasize personal qualities as determinative of success and failure and ignore discrimination and disabling social policies. The real-life stories of people with disabilities interfere with these portrayals.

The narratives of Diane DeVries and Nancy Mairs reveal a type of ordinary life that has heretofore been too often categorized

31

extraordinary. These two individuals recount their experience of painstakingly inhabiting their bodies and of disputing with society about their proper social place. In the process, they demythologize disability and refuse to acquiesce to society's stigmatization. The alternative knowledge they relate about their bodies and social relations reveals full-bodied resistance to the dominant stereotypes of people with disabilities and moves us toward a liberatory theology of disability.

Diane DeVries and Nancy Mairs embody two quite different perspectives on living disability. Because of DeVries's congenital disability, she has never internalized able-bodiedness as the norm to which she should aspire. Thus she was able to see her own body as different, but not defective. She does not "pass" or compensate socially for her disability; rather she claims her body as authentic space. Mairs, however, had lived for more than twenty-five years in a "normal" body. With the onset of the symptoms of her disability, she experienced the diminishment of her body, which she described as her body going away. Gradually she came to terms with her unfamiliar body space. Neither of these women more authentically represents the experience of people with disabilities; rather, they depict the multiple realities that constitute ordinary existence in our nonconventional bodies.

DeVries and Mairs have shared the recollections and revelations of life in their particular bodies in print. Diane DeVries collaborated with Geyla Frank, a social psychologist, in ethnographic research using DeVries's autobiography as its focal point. Their collaborative work defines the everyday world of persons with disabilities as the locus of sociological inquiry.[3] A poet and essayist, Nancy Mairs has written extensively about her experience of becoming disabled.[4] *Remembering the Bone House,* Mairs's autobiography, is a narrative of living in the "bone house" of her body. Mairs provides a complex picture of the aesthetic experience of living in a nonconventional body.

DeVries and Mairs have worked to empower other people with disabilities. DeVries has organized marches for disability rights and appeared on national news. Mairs is a well-known lecturer and advocate for disability rights and an instructor for medical interns.

These acts of resistance and solidarity are the result of making their bodies the starting point.

DIANE DEVRIES

DeVries was born in rural Texas in 1950 without lower limbs and with above-elbow upper extremity stumps. She recounts the family narrative of her birth and her own interpretation of her impairment.

> *DeVries:* When Mom was pregnant with me, they had no idea that anything was wrong, because I kicked and the whole bit, you know. And they couldn't take X rays. It was too far past that to take X rays. So they had no idea. The doctor, when I was delivered, the doctor fainted.
>
> *Frank:* Literally?
>
> *DeVries:* Literally. The nurse had to finish it. He was just out, you know. So they got me out. And I guess they probably took some test to find out, but they never did. . . .
>
> *DeVries:* But, uh, Dad believed and I do, too, that it was just something that happened. Because that's the only thing that's wrong with me, is just that I don't have no arms and legs. And they're nice and neat, too. . . . There was no other defects. Like my lungs weren't crooked or my heart wasn't, you know, up in the wrong place or something. You know. So probably it was just something that happened, I would think.[5]

What was experienced by her physician as a shocking catastrophe was viewed by DeVries as "just something that happened." As the first child in a working-class family, she portrays herself as an expected and wanted child. Nonetheless, her family moved to California shortly after her birth, in part to remove DeVries from her rejecting maternal grandmother, who accused DeVries's mother of fornicating with the devil and labeled DeVries "the devil's daughter" because of her impairment.[6] Despite the reactions of the delivering physician and her maternal grandmother, DeVries adopted the most favorable characterization of her impairment in developing the self-accepting attitude that characterizes her life.

She subscribed to her father's pragmatic interpretation of her birth as revealing the contingency of human life. In her wry dismissal of the doctor's theatrics, DeVries leaves open the question of who was the "freak." By rejecting her grandmother's belief that someone needed to be blamed for her existence, DeVries refuses to give some special explanation for her birth. It seems no more necessary to ask why she was born with her body, than it does to pose the same question of her able-bodied younger sister. In refusing to define her own birth as a tragedy, DeVries rejects dominant conceptions and reconceives it as the natural beginning of an ordinary life.

From childhood, DeVries had an accepting attitude toward her body as well. She explains that she has always been "really in tune with my body."[7] Despite others' perceptions of her physical imperfection, DeVries evaluated her body positively as compact and streamlined. Her awareness of the differences between her and others did not lead her to conclude that her body was incomplete. Although her body was different, it was, nonetheless, intact and healthy.

DeVries's evaluation of her body as unique and whole had been established before an awareness of societal stereotypes could challenge her self-image. Nonetheless, in early childhood she came to realize that for many able-bodied people her evaluation was inconceivable. She describes her first realization that her difference was evaluated as dangerous freakishness by some.

> *Frank:* How old were you when you realized that you looked different from most other people?
> *DeVries:* I realized that right away.
> *Frank:* So you always had that awareness?
> *DeVries:* Oh yeah. It never hit me one day.
> *Frank:* You never had a special awareness that outside your family people were looking at you differently?
> *DeVries:* I always knew it. It was always there because my body was so different.
> *Frank:* How did you feel about that differentness? How did you understand it?

DeVries: I just knew I was different. Certain things could happen during the day to make me sad or mad, 'cause I could go . . . weeks without it bothering me at all, because nothing happened. But something could happen, like once when I was a little kid. I was in the wagon and we were in this trailer park, and some kid came up to me with a knife. He said, "Aw, you ain't got no arms, you ain't got no legs, and now you're not gonna have no head." He held me right here, by the neck, and had a little knife. It was one of those bratty kids that did weird things. So that day, I really. . . . You know, certain times, certain things happened. Otherwise, I didn't notice.[8]

Although DeVries viewed her body as ordinary though distinct, she has been regularly exposed to hostility and differential treatment by people who interpret the absence of her limbs as monstrous. She recalls an occasion when she and a friend were moved to the front of a restaurant after being seated in the back. A waitress objected, "She'll make the people sick."[9]

DeVries experienced discrimination and marginalization in the Christian church as well. During her college years, DeVries was "born again." She and her live-in lover, later husband, joined a charismatic congregation where for several years they found acceptance and support. In 1985, DeVries related a prophecy she had received in which "the Lord told me that I was going to sing the song of the Lord and sing the prophetic."[10] Normally such a prophecy would have precipitated immediate placement in the choir. However, when DeVries approached one of the pastors about joining the choir, she received several rebuffs because of the minister's concerns to shield the congregation from her appearance, which culminated in the following conversation:

She [the pastor] said, "Well, Diane, you can't get in the choir."
And I said, "Why not?"
And she said, "Well, for one, there's a step going up to the choir."
"Yeah," I said, "You could make a ramp. Or, I could be up there already when the choir marches on."
There's a lady who's real big, really fat, and she has a hard time walking up steps, too. She's up there, before the choir gets there.

35

And I said, "Carl [her husband], he's in the choir, and a couple of other people—they, my friends, think it's really bad. . . . Carl would make sure I got up there. People would make sure I got up there."
"Oh, no," she said. "And plus that, when we all stand, and you're sitting there, that would look so awful. It would look so uneven. And what about your robe? You can't wear a big old robe."
I said, "I could get one made for me."
She said, "Oh, it just wouldn't look right."[11]

DeVries and her husband decided to leave the congregation. This experience preceded her involvement in disability rights activities, which included organizing demonstrations at the University of California at Los Angeles, where she was a student, protesting their failure to comply with Section 504 of the Rehabilitation Act of 1973 pertaining to removal of architectural barriers. Despite an accumulation of humiliating and discriminatory incidents during her lifetime, DeVries has sustained her self-definition as different and ordinary. She has developed numerous strategies for protecting herself from people's attitudes that her body is inferior and unacceptable.

DeVries's conviction that her body was whole and intact was revealed even as a young child when she rejected her rehabilitation team's efforts to persuade her to use prosthetic devices intended to "normalize" her appearance and limb function. At age five, DeVries was admitted to the Child Amputee Prosthetics Project (CAPP) at the University of California in Los Angeles. She was fitted with artificial arms and with a lower-extremity device with rocker feet. She also underwent numerous surgeries to remove bone spurs on her stumps, in order to enable her to use mechanical arms. At this stage, DeVries had little control over her medical treatment, and her parents were given limited options by her attending physicians. According to CAPP staff, DeVries could be fitted with prosthetic devices enabling her to be an independent person, or without the devices she would be relegated to lifelong dependence and institutional care. Given this incomplete and inaccurate presentation of possibilities, DeVries's parents opted to have their daughter fitted with both upper and lower prosthetic devices. From ages four to eighteen, DeVries underwent rehabilitation intended to "normalize" her functioning and make her independent.

DeVries's ambivalence about these appendages to her body thwarted the rehabilitation team's efforts at "normalization." The prosthetic arms, particularly, got in her way. Finally after twelve pairs of arms, DeVries rejected their use entirely. The prosthetic devices "were more of a hassle than a help," she reported. "Everything took longer."[12] As a child, she could color, eat and drink, and play with toys much better without the arms. DeVries felt more disabled and less independent with the devices than without them.

Although officially diagnosed as having no legs and, therefore, no ambulatory capacity, DeVries defines herself as having both legs and the ability to walk. In addition, she does not think of her walking as substantively different from conventional walking.

> *DeVries:* They discovered I had hip bones when the doctors were standing around in preparation for my first surgery. I was walking already.
> *Frank:* Walking?
> *DeVries:* Walking. On the floor. Scooting around.
> *Frank:* How?
> *DeVries:* I just moved my hips back and forth. I still do it when I have to. . . . I sit on the floor on my butt, and I move each . . . well, these, I call them legs, 'cause they are in a way. Just move each one with your hip. Just like anyone else would. Just move the top of their leg. And I got around like that. You know, around the house, not outside. . . . When I was younger, it was just my butt. But then I realized I could move each and they were separate. So they were legs, you know. I walked on them. When I was younger and thinner it was easier. I could bounce around. I used to be able to stand on my head! That amazes me when I think about it. I was really light then. They discovered I had hips and that surprised me, because I figured that if I'm walking, of course I had them.[13]

Although DeVries has rejected prosthetic devices that encumbered her rather than increased her mobility, she has incorporated functional ambulatory devices into her understanding of her intact body. She describes the battery for her electric wheelchair as "my legs" and the mobility she gains from her wheelchair as "walking."[14] In so doing, DeVries subverts the notion that she has a "natural" body and other "unnatural" accoutrements. Her body doesn't stop with the bones and flesh. She incorporates devices that promote her self-definition as a healthy, mobile, and intact woman.

DeVries's self-image is also shaped by unique social relations because of her disability. DeVries includes in her self-description images of herself dancing and running. While these images are shaped, in part, by her active imagination, they are also formed by the intimate relationship between DeVries and her able-bodied sister.

> It's true that there is a Diane within this Diane who can dance which enabled me to teach my younger sister Debbie, but there's another reason I could coach her so well. It's hard to explain. Ever since Deb could walk she was taking care of me. I saw her body move from childhood's awkwardness to adult gracefulness and strength. But not only did I see this, I felt her movements. In a sense, part of her body was mine too. So, since I knew how her body moved, I could coach her in dancing. Do you understand any of this?[15]

Her question highlights an experience she knows to be outside able-bodied categories. To suggest that she embodies not only her own, but her sister's body as well, does not fit the "normal" under-standing of the world and may sound pathological to some. Yet DeVries's experience as a woman with disabilities shapes new categories of embodiment and normality that include her percep-tion of her sister's body as a resource for constructing her own body image. DeVries drew on the physical and emotional proximity of their relationship in order to experience through connection what she could not realize independently. Her experience reveals a transformed understanding of independence, premised not on physical detachment but rather on relatedness and solidarity.

In the face of demeaning interactions and exclusionary main-stream standards for feminine attractiveness, DeVries's persistent and overriding self-image is that of a beautiful person. During

38

young adulthood, she became aware of her physical resemblance to the famous statue *Venus de Milo.*

> *DeVries:* My mother's friend one time gave her a candle of the Venus de Milo. And I came home and they lit it. I thought there was something symbolic there.
> *Frank:* Did you identify with it?
> *DeVries:* Oh yeah! I was going with a black guy named Rico and I gave him a big statue of the Venus de Milo for his birthday. He loved it. . . . It was pretty, too.
> *Frank:* She's an image of you, really. She doesn't have legs.
> *DeVries:* And also the one arm is shorter than the other. That's what's so weird, too. Also, Diane is Greek. Or Roman. Diane is the other name for Venus.[16]

Although DeVries is mistaken about the mythology (Venus was the goddess of beauty and love; her Greek name was Aphrodite), what is important is her self-definition as a woman of rare beauty. Like the *Venus de Milo,* whose beauty was apparent not in spite of but precisely because of her unconventional body, DeVries presents her body as attractive, whole, and integrated, claiming an empowering image that reinforces her self-understanding.

DeVries's experience and presentation of her body confound dominant notions of ordinary, natural, independence, and beauty. From childhood, she acted upon a conviction that her different body was not abnormal. Although repeatedly confronted with humiliating and sometimes violent reminders of her difference, she rejected medical and social prescriptions intended to "normalize" her by camouflaging her body. DeVries has experienced many, if not most, of the ordinary life events for an individual of her age, gender, and social background. She was reared at home with her family, went to public schools, had an active social life, lived with friends, had lovers, graduated from university, lived on her own, joined a church and left it, became pregnant, married, and divorced.[17] She has also lived in institutions for people with disabilities, attended special schools, used prostheses and abandoned them, undergone numerous surgeries, and relied upon attendant care. She has lived an ordinary life in an unconventional body.

39

DeVries's self-definition also ignores determinations of natural and unnatural experience. Her incorporation of mobility-enhancing devices into her body image redefines normal embodiment. DeVries's use of social and emotional connection for defining her body suggests an alternative practice of the relation between independence and solidarity. Finally, DeVries models physical beauty, thereby subverting dominant standards that would permit her only "inner beauty." By defining and valuing her own body, DeVries places herself at the social center.

NANCY MAIRS

Nancy Mairs was diagnosed with multiple sclerosis at age twenty-nine, just after she moved to Tucson, Arizona, to begin graduate school in creative writing. Her essays and poetry detail an acknowledgment of her metamorphosing body. She has not overcome disability and the body pain that it entails; rather, she has come to her body, tolerating its limitations and doing what she can.

> A reviewer once spoke of my "valiant battle against multiple sclerosis." It was a bad review, but I hated this phrase—which I suspect he meant as a compliment—far more than the nastiness he dispensed. I hated the way he reduced the existence I have painstakingly constructed to the corpses and smoking rubble of a battlefield and set me, a heroic figure, wounded but still defiant, in the middle of the waste. . . . Lest you be tempted into similar maudlin misreading of life with chronic illness, keep this in mind: I am only doing what I have to do. It's enough.[18]

Although her disability came unexpected and unwanted, Mairs has utilized it as a creative resource, becoming intensely aware of the work her body does in her writing. For Mairs, this accessibility to her body is an ambiguous position, revealing both weakness and strength. Her body both gets in the way of creativity and is a conduit for it.

When she began to realize that she was a body in trouble, Mairs was a married woman with two children. Her life was interwoven with those of her husband, daughter and son, as well as lovers, in-laws, mother, and stepfather. She sketches the complexity of social relations that impinge on an individual's experience of disease and disability. She becomes very clear that a body, perhaps especially a disabled body, is not a space one occupies alone.

Her writing chronicles her different dealings with her body and this degenerative disease. Her initial response to MS was a belief that "even the little I have will ultimately be taken away."[19]

> My body
> is going away.
>
> It fades
> to the transparency
> of rubbed amber
> held against the
>   sun.
>
> It shrinks.
> It grows quiet.
>
> Small, quiet,
> it is a cold
> and heavy
> smoothed stone.
>
> Who will have it
> When it lies
> pale and polished
> as a clean bone?[20]

She expressed her fury at the inevitability of disability through a tremendous passion for bodily experience. An "electrical storm spitting sparks of sexuality," Mairs was intent on proving her autonomy.[21] Prodded by her rebel body, she moved out of the house she had shared with her able-bodied husband and children.

> The house itself is too big for me now. I'm too weak to care
> for it properly, and no one else is willing, so I feel constantly

41

as though it's falling down around my ears. I can't breathe here. . . . I run away from home. Not far. About nine blocks. I find one little room. . . . I like its snugness, as though it were a ship's cabin or a camper, something miniature, encompassable, to carry me along.[22]

In this space, she broke down and attempted suicide. "The fact that I'm having a breakdown strikes me abruptly and with perfect clarity. I go on having the breakdown anyway."[23] There was no safe space for Mairs during this time. Her body had betrayed her; the expansiveness of her house smothered her; and even the apartment to which she fled dislodged her. She lived out her ordeal of disability—that there will be no physical space for her. Nancy Mairs does not spare her readers the panic and refuses to allow them to believe that MS really is not as bad as all that, nor does she confirm society's suspicions about people with disabilities by dissolving into helplessness in her pain. Mairs ferociously tried to settle herself in comfortable space.

After nearly a year of depression and roaming, Mairs recognized that although her body was changing, it was doing so at a slower pace than she had anticipated. She could not expend herself in a frenzy and be done with it. This body was going to be with her for a long time. She would have to conceive a body that was both habitable and inhospitable—a body of plenty and privation.

My world has, of necessity, been circumscribed by my losses, but the terrain left me has been ample enough for me to continue many of the activities that absorb me: writing, teaching, raising children and cats and plants and snakes, speaking publicly about MS and depression, even playing bridge with people patient and honorable enough to let me scatter cards every which way without sneaking a peek.[24]

The boundaries of living disability became routine. She could live this way. She wrote about the change and compromise and was surprised at the normality and the humor that continued to accompany life in her nonconventional body. "I lead, on the whole, an ordinary life probably rather like the one I would have led had I not had MS."[25]

Slowly Mairs discovered that her body was not going away at all; rather it was being incorporated (becoming a body) for the first time. She gained an awareness of her body that she had never had before. She could no longer take her physical existence for granted; by necessity, she had to pay attention to the placement of her feet, to raising herself from the toilet seat, to lifting her coffee cup. The concentration on these ordinary tasks previously performed unselfconsciously opened a world of space to her. She began to realize the ways in which she was formed by the place her body takes in the world. In 1989, she published her autobiography retracing the spaces she has occupied throughout her life. Her work goes a long way in concretely breaking the mind-body dualism that has been the norm for literary production. She deconstructs the heroic tale of conquering bodies, substituting instead her realistically powerful body.

> Now I am who I will be. A body in trouble. I've spent all these years trying alternately to repudiate and to control my wayward body, to transcend it one way or another, but MS rams me right back down into it. "The body," I've gotten into the habit of calling it. "The left leg is weak," I say. "There's a blurred spot in the right eye." As though it were some other entity, remote and traitorous. Or worse, as though it were inanimate, a prison of bone, the dark tower around which Childe Roland rode, withershins left, withershins right, seeking to free the fair kidnapped princess: me. My favorite fairy tale as a child turns out to have nothing to offer my adulthood. Rescue from the body is merely another word for death.
> Slowly, slowly, MS will teach me to live on as a body.[26]

For Mairs, incorporation takes on a variety of meanings. It signifies acknowledgment of her nonconventional body, but it also means encompassing artificial body parts that compose her "bones and braces body." As she acquired braces, canes, and electric scooters, she came to realize that her body was emerging as she went along.

> The brace makes my MS concrete and forces me to wear it on the outside. As soon as I strapped the brace on, I climbed into

43

trousers and stayed there (though not in the same trousers, of course). The idea of going around with my bare brace hanging out seemed almost as indecent as exposing my breasts. Not until 1984, soon after I won the Western States Book Award for poetry, did I put on a skirt short enough to reveal my plasticized leg. The connection between winning a writing award and baring my brace is not merely fortuitous; being affirmed as a writer really did embolden me. Since then, I've grown so accustomed to wearing skirts that I don't think about my brace any more than I think about my cane. I've incorporated them, I suppose: made them, in their necessity, insensate but fundamental parts of my body.[27]

Incorporation also means conceiving a corpus—a collection of writing. Mairs's carnal essays are not stories about a self or a soul, but embodied prose. She intends her work as "reclaiming human experience, insofar as I can find it embodied in my own experience, from the morass of secrecy and shame into which Christian and pre-Christian social taboos have plunged it, to rescue and restore God's good creation."[28] In service of that desire, she tries "to keep as close to the bone of my experience as I can."[29] This tangible metaphor provides a useful image of her disability as a means of accessing the world and herself.

I've "found" my voice, then, just where it ought to have been, in the body-warmed breath escaping my lungs and throat. Forced by the exigencies of physical disease to embrace my self in the flesh, I couldn't write bodiless prose. The voice is the creature of the body that produces it. I speak as a crippled woman. At the same time, in the utterance I redeem both "cripple" and "woman" from the shameful silences by which I have often felt surrounded, contained, set apart; I give myself permission to live openly among others, to reach out for them, stroke them with fingers and sighs. No body, no voice; no voice, no body. That's what I know in my bones.[30]

Her descriptions and embodied self-revelations disclose disability as part of an ordinary life. Mairs plumbs the social fears that "this could happen to me" by acknowledging that it well could. She offers few soothing words to those who would shield themselves from their bodies. For her readers, as for her, the chaos nears and panic churns. Carefully she moves toward the realization she can live in her "crippled" body and urges her reader to accompany her. For her, as for many people with disabilities, this is an ambiguous discovery. It means days of lumbering, plodding, punching through life. This is not self-pity; it is realism.

This commitment to realism also disallows that she or her husband be portrayed as heroic. She places alongside the comments about the supposed saintliness of a husband who would stand by her despite her affairs and her disability the reality of their marriage which also has involved his affairs and emotional absence, frustrating the search for the heroic sufferer either in the person with disabilities or in caregivers.[31] Suffering, she contends, has few heroes, least of all those who wish to live ordinary lives.

Mairs's conversion to Catholicism, which she relates in *Ordinary Time*, is a conversion of body, begun in the real presence of those who call her to herself and to others. Her turning toward God is a process of settling into the Body of Christ, acknowledging the tensions of being both Catholic and feminist and expressing her criticisms of the institutional church. Her conversion to the poor, afflicted, and oppressed also necessitates a habit of "turning toward and taking in" their real, lived experiences.[32] Her conversion hence requires recognizing her own need for mercy.

> I cannot patronize the poor. I am one of the poor. Currently my poverty isn't economic, though it may one day be that as well, but its effects are similar. I must be not only the agent but the object of the works of mercy. I must discipline myself to accept and welcome other's care. I wish I could tell you that I'm doing a terrific job of it, that I'm just the sweetest, humblest little woman you've ever met, but I can't. All I can say is that, in learning to give whenever I can and receive care whenever I must, I've grown more attentive to the personal dimension of the works of mercy.[33]

Difficulty and doing things the hard way have their uses, Mairs has discovered. She found "how I can not merely admit to having a difficult life but also use the difficulties I've acknowledged to enrich the life."[34] These horrible things need not diminish us; they can make us more fully aware of the full range of things human. Performing an authentic alchemy using disability and honesty, Mairs has fashioned a difficult life, in contrast to our constant search for ease and painlessness. Her difficult life need not be denied or descried. It need only be lived. "Because a difficult life is more complicated than an easy one, it offers opportunities for developing a greater range of response to experience: a true generosity of spirit."[35] It also opens a space for honesty about death as part of an ordinary life. Mairs writes, "Taught through intimate relations with disability and death that life, though lugubrious enough, is even more ludicrous and that no one develops fully until she can play and mourn in balance, I had to risk a messenger's death then and still must do: We *are* all going to die. And it is all right."[36]

Recognizing and coming to terms with the difficulty that comes with disability, Mairs lives not with the grace of a martyr but with the resolve of someone who realizes that an ordinary life is filled with blessings and curses and that it is sometimes hard to differentiate between the two.

> All the same, if a cure were found, would I take it? In a minute. I may be a cripple, but I'm only occasionally a loony and never a saint. Anyway, in my brand of theology God doesn't give bonus points for a limp. I'd take a cure; I just don't need one. A friend who also has MS startled me once by asking, "Do you ever say to yourself, 'Why me, Lord?'" "No, Michael, I don't," I told him, "because whenever I try, the only response I can think of is 'Why not?'" If I could make a cosmic deal, who would I put in my place? What in my life would I give up in exchange for sound limbs and a thrilling rush of energy? No one. Nothing. I might as well do the job myself. Now that I am getting the hang of it.[37]

TOWARD A LIBERATORY THEOLOGY:
THEMES FROM OUR LIVES

Diane DeVries and Nancy Mairs witness to the alternative perspectives embodied by people with disabilities. These bodies of knowledge provide a primary source for the development of a liberatory theology of disability. In their narratives, three liberatory themes, in particular, emerged. First, both women reveal in their bodies the reality that ordinary lives incorporate contingency and difficulty. Furthermore, they embody this contingency and difficulty not only with anger and disappointment but also with respect for its unique value. Too often acknowledgment of vulnerability by people with disabilities has led to overemphasis on powerlessness and suffering. Yet as these narratives make clear the expression of grief is fundamentally different from the pronouncement of tragedy. For both women grief sometimes accompanied their efforts to live ordinary lives. Yet the identification between disability and tragedy fails to correspond to the complex array of experiences revealed in the narratives of Mairs and DeVries. On the contrary, their real, lived experiences highlight physical contingency as a frequent source of creativity and of uncommon experiences of interrelationship.

Second, the narratives highlight an alternative understanding of embodiment, recognizing it as an intricate interweaving of physical sensations and emotional attachments, irrespective of socially constructed notions of "normal" bodies or "appropriate" relations. DeVries and Mairs include as integral parts of their bodies braces and wheelchairs. Both rely on close relationships to increase their own sense of body. Their experiences reveal painstaking processes of putting themselves together using whatever resources that are available. In contrast to romantic notions of "natural" embodiment, both discuss embodying technology. Some devices, for example, wheelchairs and braces, are integrated into their body awareness, while other appliances that frustrate their sense of body are rejected.

This alternative understanding of embodiment suggests that embodiment is a social accomplishment, achieved through attentiveness to the needs, limits, and bounty of the body in relation to others. It recognizes that limits are real human facts and that heroism cannot eliminate some limits. It encompasses the recognition that disability does not mean incomplete and that difference is not dangerous. Embodying disability is not an extraordinary feat;

47

rather it too is a process of symbolically and corporeally constructing wholeness and ordinary physicality. This notion differs significantly from those understandings of embodiment that relate to ideas about normality and naturalness.

Finally, the narratives identify disability as part of an ordinary life while attesting to the real differences between people with disabilities and the able-bodied and combating false and oppressive explanations of the nature of those differences. Both women accurately distinguish between the physical contingency that is part of ordinary life and socially constructed barriers that make ordinary life impossible; and both demonstrate self-valuation and struggle for justice in the face of persistent discrimination and devaluation. Resistance as self-valuation is revealed in DeVries's identification of an empowering image attesting to her physical beauty and Mairs's determination to engage in productive work despite barriers. Resistance as the struggle for justice necessitated that both women tell the truth about their experiences of disability in all their complexity and ambivalence, and it led to their work as activists.

The individual narratives of people with disabilities must be tied to the larger story of the development and evolution of the community of people with disabilities. In chapter 3, I chronicle the social movement for disability rights, recognition, and participation. Further, I examine a shift in the sociology of disability in which the person with disabilities becomes the subject, rather than the object of inquiry. This shift has been linked to the emergence of the disability rights movement and continues to offer a theoretical construct for empowerment and liberation for people with disabilities.

CHAPTER THREE

THE BODY POLITICS

The "body"—of individuals and the body of populations—appears as the bearer of new variables, not merely as between the scarce and the numerous and the submissive and the restive, rich and poor, healthy and sick, strong and weak, but also as between the more or less utilisable, more or less amenable to profitable investment, those with greater or lesser prospects of survival, death and illness, and with more or less capacity for being usefully trained.

Michel Foucault[1]

For persons with disabilities, the body is the center of political struggle. In challenging society's definitions of our bodies as flawed, dangerous, and dependent, people with disabilities initiated a social movement that stressed positive self-image and self-help. The movement has grown as we have refused to allow our bodies to be warehoused in institutions, restricted from public buildings, and discriminated against in employment. People with disabilities in recent years have become increasingly visible and active in public life.

The existence of this new "body" of people with disabilities facilitated, in turn, a paradigm shift within the sociology of disability. In the 1940s and 1950s, studies of people with disabilities were generally conducted under the rubric of deviance analysis. This literature focused on the limitations of people with disabilities and tended to attribute our lack of social participation to an inability to cope physically, emotionally, or socially. Yet as people with disabilities gained the power to define our experiences in society, a new sociological paradigm began to emerge that shifted focus

49

from problem individuals to the social problem of the exclusion of people with disabilities as a group. This reorientation is most clearly epitomized in the minority-group model of social analysis that has fostered research into the social difficulties and structural inequalities confronted by disabled persons.

This chapter gives a brief historical overview of the social movement of people with disabilities in the United States and a summary of the dominant sociological interpretations of disability. In particular, the shift from medical and economic definitions of disability to a sociopolitical one will be noted. This new sociological paradigm provides resources for new theological conceptions of disability, as well. Recognition of the sociopolitical dimensions of physical disability is vital if we hope to restructure and reconceive contemporary theology about disability and to ground a liberatory theology of disability in the individual and collective bodies of people with disabilities.

NEW BODIES: VETERANS AND CHILDREN WITH DISABILITIES

The genesis of a social movement of people with disabilities in the United States must be traced, in part, to the politics of war. Prior to World Wars I and II, people with disabilities were, for the most part, cared for by families and private disability-specific institutions, segregated and hidden from mainstream society. After each war, however, the return of disabled veterans heightened public awareness and increased governmental involvement in providing for the financial and medical needs of people with disabilities.

The first federal legislation to address the specific needs of people with disabilities was the Smith-Sears Veterans' Rehabilitation Act of 1918, which authorized a program of vocational training for disabled veterans.[2] Although such legislation sought to aid veterans with disabilities, inefficiencies in disbursement and implementation often delayed or nullified federal assistance. In the wake of governmental inaction, these veterans founded advocacy groups to promote their causes before federal and state agencies, to provide mutual support, and to educate the public. The Disabled American Veterans (DAV), one of the earliest self-advocacy groups for people with disabilities, was founded in 1920 by World War I veterans. Throughout its history, the DAV focused on expanding government benefits for disabled veterans and providing counseling for individual members.[3] Other veterans' organizations, including Paralyzed American Veterans (PAV), founded after World War II, also sought to advance the position of their specific constituencies.

In addition to disabled veterans, another population of persons with disabilities increased dramatically from the 1940s to the 1960s—children with disabilities. The "Baby Boom" coupled with changing patterns in infant mortality meant that there were more children generally as well as more children with congenital disabilities needing services. Likewise, the polio epidemics in the early 1950s and the thalidomide poisoning in the late 1950s and early 1960s left many young people and children disabled.[4]

Public awareness of children with disabilities spawned the growth of philanthropic organizations that sought access to education and adequate medical treatment on behalf of these children. For example, the Easter Seal Society, founded in the 1940s (later the Easter Seal Society for Crippled Children and Adults), established educational and medical institutions for the care of children and young adults with disabilities. Other advocacy groups, led by parents of children with disabilities, also struggled to increase the educational services and opportunities available to children with mental and physical disabilities.

MANAGED BODIES: VOCATIONAL AND MEDICAL REHABILITATION

These new populations of veterans and children with disabilities led to a concomitant expansion of the rehabilitation professions and facilities. Although the history of rehabilitation policy and implementation will not be recounted here, an abridged account of its definitional influence is vital for understanding the shape of today's disability rights movement.[5] The overriding goal of reha-

51

bilitation was "getting a person back to work, assisting him [or her] to achieve maximum independence, improving his [or her]self-image, and imbuing the disabled and the public with an increased respect for human life," according to Gary Albrecht, a medical sociologist.[6] Although the intent was clearly worthwhile and the practice has aided many individuals, the rehabilitation paradigm has had, at best, mixed results for many people with disabilities.

Rehabilitation as practiced was divided institutionally into two emphases, vocational training and placement and medical intervention. These goals fostered alternative definitions of the nature of disability and determined the range of services available to people with disabilities. Vocational rehabilitation policy initiatives treated disability in predominantly economic terms, that is, as an inability to work in one's former employment or as a health-related limitation on the amount or kind of work a person could perform.[7] Hence federal and state rehabilitation services functioned much like an employment agency for people with disabilities that provided training, employment counseling, and job contacts.

This practice of conflating disability and unemployability presumed that persons with disabilities were distinguished primarily by an inability to perform a particular socially valuable activity, for example, financially compensated work. Because of this working definition of disability, vocational rehabilitation has been particularly inadequate in addressing the needs of many women with disabilities who work in the home. Despite the positive emphases on education and employment, vocational rehabilitation proposed an incomplete agenda for remedying the disadvantages confronting people with disabilities. For example, regardless of their qualifications, people with disabilities are regularly denied opportunities for employment because of attitudinal and architectural barriers. These obstacles to employment are not addressed by educating people with disabilities.

Medical rehabilitation, on the other hand, classified disability as chiefly a medical problem. Rehabilitative specialists responded to the increased demand for innovative services from the new body of people with disabilities and to the greater willingness of insurance companies to compensate physicians for such treatment. The treatment of physical disabilities became a medical speciality guided by medical diagnoses and requiring new therapeutic institutions.

Under the aegis of designing comprehensive medical rehabilitation programs, hospitals and physicians began to incorporate rehabilitation services into the medical model. Definitions of disabling conditions and appropriate treatments were expanded to include medical intervention and physician control.[8]

The medical treatment model of rehabilitation, though it resulted in critical medical advances for people with disabilities, also was incomplete in that it, too, failed to address social aspects of disability, including poverty and isolation. Furthermore, medical rehabilitation substituted professional control for the individual self-determination of people with disabilities.

The negative impact of the medical/rehabilitation model lies in its perpetuation of the dependent and nonparticipatory role expected of the "patient" in regard to decisions about "illness" and its negative impact in defining the role of disabled people in virtually every aspect of life, from education and employment to transportation and voting.[9]

People with disabilities were encouraged to accept their limitations, as a part of the rehabilitation process, and to view themselves as dependent on medical care. Both the medical and the vocational rehabilitation models participated in and supported the prevailing belief that the problem of disability was fundamentally the problem of individuals and was best addressed by treatment, employment, or education.

POLITICAL BODIES: THE GROWTH OF A CIVIL RIGHTS MOVEMENT

Although the emergence of the disability rights movement in the late 1960s and early 1970s was the result of many factors, it must be interpreted, in part, as a response to the deficiencies of the vocational and medical rehabilitation approaches to disability.[10] In contrast to the economic and medical models of disability, disabil-

53

ity rights activists advanced a sociopolitical perspective that highlighted legislative redress of discrimination and fostered an emphasis on independent living and self-advocacy.

The independent living movement resulted in the establishment
of the first Centers for Independent Living (CIL) in California and
other cities across the United States in the 1960s. Circumventing the
near absolute control over essential services wielded by governmental
agencies and medical institutions, these CILs acted as clearing-
houses for information on housing, transportation, and education
and facilitated direct contact with attendants and other service
providers. Their philosophy asserted that

> 1. Those who best know the needs of disabled people and how
> to meet those needs are disabled people themselves. 2. The
> needs of the disabled can be met most effectively by comprehen-
> sive programs which provide a variety of services. 3. Disabled
> people should be integrated as fully as possible into their com-
> munity.[11]

These centers, founded in numerous university communities
across the United States, also cultivated a national network of
youthful activists who, although they arose mainly from certain
disability groups, including muscular dystrophy, spinal cord injuries, multiple sclerosis, and cerebral palsy, advocated a common
sociopolitical agenda opposing social exclusion and discrimination, in addition to their disability-specific concerns.

Another key factor in the emergence of the disability rights
movement was a new generation of socially active young people
with disabilities. This generation included large numbers of new
groups of people with disabilities, for example, those who had been
disabled during childhood or young adulthood and those with
congenital disabilities who had been reared in middle-class families. Richard Scotch, a leading sociologist of disability, writes:

> Most individuals who experienced disability as the result of
> polio, teenage automobile or diving accidents, or the Vietnam
> War had clear memories of themselves as nondisabled, and
> many retained expectations of full economic and social partici-

pation. . . . Even for children whose disabilities came at birth and who grew up in the 1950s and 1960s, individual potential was stressed by the Spock-influenced middle-class parents of that affluent era, who promoted self-confidence and achievement in their children.[12]

Personal expectations of social participation translated into political goals as these young people with disabilities met on campuses teeming with political activism during the 1960s and 1970s. Schooled in the tactics of self-advocacy and grass-roots organizing, these young activists founded a plethora of local organizations from Disabled in Action (DIA) in New York City to WARPATH (World Association to Remove Prejudice Against the Handicapped) in Florida.[13]

A third critical impetus for the disability rights movement was the diffusion of civil rights ideas in the wake of the struggle for civil rights by African Americans, women, and other racial minorities. In light of previous victories won by these minority groups, people with disabilities increasingly identified themselves as subject to discrimination as a social group on the basis of disability. This orientation called into question the prevailing attitude that access and public services for people with disabilities were a matter of societal benevolence, asserting instead that people with disabilities have a civil right to access in societal institutions and public resources. It also began to dislodge the individualistic notions of disability.

However, these organizations and the escalating impulse for civil rights needed institutional support in order to encourage a national civil rights movement among people with disabilities. The unwitting facilitating organization was the President's Committee on the Employment of the Handicapped (PCEH). Founded after World War II, PCEH was controlled by service providers who advocated the traditional emphases on vocational training and medical rehabilitation. Yet the annual meetings also attracted younger activists with civil rights agendas who formed a loose network that offered alternative workshops and organized the first national coalition of advocacy organizations, the American Coalition of Citizens with Disabilities (ACCD). This organization became a major coordinating network of disability rights groups through the 1970s and a leading advocate for integrating civil rights guarantees for people with disabilities into federal laws and regulations.[14]

As the disability movement gained numerical strength and national status, it intensified its efforts in Washington, D.C. Beginning in the 1960s and continuing during the 1970s, governmental agencies and officials, as well as the general public, were made aware of the barriers confronting people with disabilities. This awareness eventually translated into the passage of legislation, beginning with the Architectural Barriers Act of 1968, which required the removal of architectural barriers from new federally funded buildings. During 1973 and 1974 in particular, significant legislative gains were made for civil rights. Section 504 of the Rehabilitation Act of 1973 was the first legislation to guarantee people with disabilities the right of access to federally funded programs; the Education for All Handicapped Children Act of 1975 ensured a free and appropriate public education and related service to children regardless of handicapping condition, in the least restrictive environment.[15]

These laws not only increased accessibility to public education, employment, government services, and public facilities, they also reinforced views of disability that highlighted the existence of a minority group whose commonality was exclusion and discrimination on the basis of disability. This legislative trend culminated in the passage of the Americans with Disabilities Act of 1990, which asserts that the 43,000,000 Americans who are disabled "are a discrete and insular minority who have been faced with restrictions and limitations, subjected to a history of purposeful unequal treatment, and relegated to a position of political powerlessness in our society."[16]

This explicit public acknowledgment of the minority status of people with disabilities has been a significant breakthrough for the disability rights movement and represents real progress for social equality. This minority-group definition also underscores an alternative theoretical approach to the sociological analysis of disability. Just as in recent decades the sociological study of race or gender has been influenced by and influential in the civil rights movements of African Americans and women, so too have the social scientific models of disability and the disability rights movement been reciprocally related.

BODIES IN SOCIETY: SOCIOLOGICAL PARADIGMS OF DISABILITY

The social scientific study of disability has progressed within three interrelated but conceptually distinct categories of analysis, namely, that of the individual psyche, that of micro-societal inter-action, and that of the social group. In what follows, representative and influential theoretical paradigms for each of the categories are briefly introduced and evaluated. The transition from individual-istic to social group definitions of disability will be apparent in the analyses. As social scientists began to address the existence of a body of people with disabilities, the inadequacies of paradigms that focused primarily on the psychological state or functional limita-tions of disabled individuals became evident.

The rise of the social scientific study of disability in the United States was facilitated in the 1940s by the Social Science Research Council's Committee on Social Adjustment. The committee was particularly interested in discovering practical means for facilitat-ing psychological adjustment to physical disability. Its attention centered on the physical deviance of persons with disabilities and their concomitant inability to conform to socially prescribed tasks and roles.[17] The goal of adjustment was closely linked with the ascendant field of rehabilitation. These scholars assumed that individuals with disabilities must undergo medical treatment and physical rehabilitation as well as a process of psychological adjust-ment in coming to terms with disability.[18] They posited the exist-ence of a stable pattern for this adjustment and believed that people with disabilities could be guided through stages to a well-adjusted state, usually as defined by able-bodied researchers or rehabilitation specialists.

While this theoretical model has evolved in the past fifty years, the primary focus remains essentially the same—the disabled indi-

57

vidual's psychological process of adjustment. This model, still held by some social scientists and many laypersons, continues to frame disability as an individual dilemma instead of as a social predicament and hence a political problem. This concentration on the individual psyche perpetuates the isolation of physical disability and fails to transform hidden, individual difficulties into a shared awareness of their meaning as social problems, to facilitate our expressions of frustration and calls for justice, and to reveal our hidden history.

Although the relationship between physical disability and an individual's self-concept is a critical topic for social scientific investigation, the theoretical paradigm of adjustment provides too static and simplistic an account of this relationship. From the perspective of theory, research simply does not support the existence of a single pattern of adjustment among people with disabilities.[19] Individuals with disabilities demonstrate wide variability in their responses to disability and often experience renewed distress long after adjustment has supposedly taken place. Irving Zola, a sociologist with disabilities, criticized the personal implications of the approach.

> I realized how meager are our attempts to write and do research about adjustment and adaptation. It would be nice if, at some point, growing up ends and maturity begins, or if one could say that successful adjustment and adaptation to a particular difficulty had been achieved. For most problems, or perhaps most basic life issues, there is no single time for such a resolution to occur. The problems must be faced, evaluated, re-defined, and readapted to, again and again and again.[20]

Although living with disability is unique to each individual, it is shaped by a dominant social milieu that devalues and discriminates against people with disabilities. Purely psychological conceptions of adjustment fail to provide a framework that enables people with disabilities to detect in our personal experiences the effects of a society-wide structure of marginalization and discrimination.

The micro-societal interactionist analysis of disability, exemplified by Erving Goffman's influential theory of stigma, represents a significant advance on the purely psychological conceptions of adjustment. Goffman presented his theory of stigma within a theoretical framework that likened social action to the performance of theatrical roles. He noted that people, like actors on a stage, manage social cues to create and sustain an impression of who they are and what they are doing all the time. Some people, however, are cast in roles that constrain their capacity to manage positive impressions of themselves. These people are stigmatized; that is, they are marked as bearers of what Goffman identified as a "spoiled identity."[21]

Goffman asserted that stigmas are socially constructed relationships. Historically, stigmas were imposed on individuals in the form of physical marking or branding to disgrace them. In modern societies, however, stigmas arise through social processes of interaction whereby individuals are marked or segregated because of an attribute they possess or because of something discrediting known about them. Hence stigmatized identities emerge through interpersonal interactions rather than as a psychological reaction to events.

According to Goffman, the stigma serves as the dominant status, determining the nature of the stigmatized person's interactions with others and accounting for the negative, prejudicial aspect of the majority's reaction to those who are different. Such an individual is recast—not as whole and normal but as tainted and alien. Because of his emphasis on an individual's efforts to manage impressions, Goffman stressed the importance of the visibility of the stigma, noting that visibility affects the general awareness of stigma in interaction and, thereby, the extent to which the nonstigmatized individual will treat the stigmatic person differently. Goffman's theory contended that the extent to which the possessor is held responsible for her or his condition varies according to the type of stigma. For example, while a paraplegic may be deemed an innocent victim, a convicted felon may not. Despite variations in perceived culpability, all stigmatic individuals possess a trait that makes them different from normals, whom Goffman defined as "those who do not depart negatively from the particular expectations at issue."[22]

The mere existence of stigma ensures that social interactions between stigmatized and nonstigmatized persons are usually uncomfortable, tense, and frustrating. Goffman hypothesized that in order to reduce this interaction anxiety, the stigmatized person frequently attempts to pass as normal or cover the immediate impact of physical difference. "Passing," however, often fails and results in unpredictable, embarrassing incidents through which the stigma is revealed and the pretense of normality is laid bare. Blocked from normal interaction, the stigmatized individual seeks to use her or his stigma for "secondary gains," to see the stigma as a blessing in disguise, or to reassess the limitation of normals.[23]

Writing in the early 1960s, Goffman claimed that "separate systems of honor"—meaning subcultures of group definition and valuation—seemed to be declining in the United States. He proposed as a "pivotal fact" that the stigmatized individual "tends to hold the same beliefs about identity that we [the normal majority] do."[24] Goffman asserted that once a person becomes aware of her or his stigmatized label, self-perceptions are affected. Even if the person rejects the label, that person will participate in a set of altered social relations presupposed by the stigma. Stigmatized individuals assimilate the values of the dominant group.

Goffman's stature within social scientific circles and the originality of his insights propelled his conceptual framework of stigma to become the dominant framework for interpreting the experience of disability. Unfortunately, while it offered the possibility of broader social analysis of the experience of the stigmatized person, his theory continued to address the problem of disability primarily as a micro-social and virtually individual one. One theorist noted that although Goffman was concerned with social surroundings, interactions, and processes, his theory of stigma was in the end reducible to the individual.[25] Whereas the adjustment model located the problem of disability in the disabled individual's psyche, Goffman's stigma paradigm located it in the body of the person with disabilities and the social disruption his or her presence initiates.

Other researchers have suggested that Goffman's episodic descriptions of the effects of stigma hinder a systematic understanding of how stigma operates throughout the stigmatized person's lifetime and in long-term interaction.[26] Goffman's theory of stigma freezes the isolated stigmatized person in perpetual introductions and initial conversations.

> He deals mainly with single individuals in brief encounters with normals, usually in 'unfocussed gatherings'. He seems less concerned with patients' efforts toward destigmatisation in more permanent groups, especially in social settings where they live together in more or less continuous interaction, where they are able to develop their own subculture, norms and ideology, and where they possess some measure of control over penetrating dissonany and discrediting views from without.[27]

Although the theory of stigma does highlight the interpersonal practices of social relations, it ignores the institutional practices that undergird them. For example, it can be argued that it was the social practice of secluding people with disabilities in segregated institutions that promoted infrequent and, therefore, awkward and tense interaction between individuals with disabilities and normals. Goffman's theory of stigma may provide a metaphor to illustrate what happens to individuals with disabilities in social interaction, but it fails to explain why this stigmatization occurs or to explore collective in addition to individual responses to stigma.

Goffman's critics also challenge his assumption that there is congruence between the disvalued status of the stigmatized person and that person's self-valuation. According to one researcher, Goffman "doomed the deviants of his hypothetical population to eternal stigmatization in their own eyes as well as those of society by his premise that the stigmatized apparently accept the very norms that disqualify them."[28] For example, Goffman's conclusion that a single structure of valuation holds sway over all social interaction failed to account for the mounting demands for equality of opportunity made by minority groups who were disadvantaged because of discrimination based on race and disability. The advancement of civil rights subcultures, contemporaneous to his writing, was absent from Goffman's analysis. His assertion that stigmatized persons will not accept different systems of valuation if they become available within a society was simply counterfactual.

The social group category of analysis offers new conceptual frameworks to account for the emergence of an alternative system of valuation embraced by people with disabilities, to consider people with disabilities as a distinct segment of society, and to analyze the relationship of people with disabilities as a group to the able-bodied majority. The minority-group model holds that the physical and psychological restrictions that people with disabilities face are primarily due to prejudice and social discrimination, and only secondarily to the functional limitations or emotional disturbance related to our physical impairments. Hence the locus of the problem of disability is neither the psyches nor the bodies of individuals with disabilities, but rather it is the system of social relations and institutions that has accomplished the marginalization of people with disabilities as a group.

The minority-group model was articulated as early as 1948 by social psychologist Roger Barker, who wrote:

> The minority status of the physically disabled which is due to the negative attitudes of the physically normal majority . . . would seem to be in almost all respects similar to the problem of racial and religious underprivileged minorities. . . . When and as these problems are solved with respect to these other underprivileged minorities, the solutions may be applied to the physically handicapped as well.[29]

Although Barker proposed a nascent minority model of disability, his professional concentration on a somatopsychology, that is, a social psychology of physique, emphasized the deviant physical characteristics of disabled individuals more than the intransigent social structures and attitudes. Hence the minority-model languished as a scholarly interpretation of physical disability. In the past twenty years, however, as the sociopolitical movement for disability rights expanded, the minority-group approach again gained attention. Many scholars of disability have since attempted to develop a minority-group analysis of disability issues and disability experiences.[30]

The minority-group paradigm relies on the definition of a minority group as "a group of people, who because of their physical or cultural characteristics, are singled out from others in the society in which they live for differential and unequal treatment, and who therefore regard themselves as objects of collective discrimination."[31] One elaboration of the minority model highlights the following criteria for designating a minority group: (1) The majority group subordinates the minority group, and accompanies this with prejudice and pejorative treatment of minority group members. (2) The minority group is so classified because of an identifiable, "socially important" characteristic common to all its members. (3) Minority group members are aware of themselves as a group. (4) Minority group members usually do not voluntarily join the group. (5) Intra-group marriage is the norm and is encouraged by both the majority and the minority groups.[32]

Confirmation of the minority group status of people with disabilities can be obtained by simply substituting "people with disabilities" for references to minority group members in the preceding sentences. People with disabilities are subjected to prejudicial attitudes and discriminatory acts by the able-bodied majority, who consider people with disabilities inferior and use environmental segregation by way of built architectural barriers, as means of keeping a social and physical distance.[33] A prime example is colleges and universities that ostensibly admit academically qualified people with disabilities yet do not provide specialized facilities or necessary services, thus making matriculation for these students exceptionally difficult. Simply ignoring the special needs of people with disabilities constitutes discrimination.

Although the etiology of disabilities, their visibility, and the degree of functional impairment varies dramatically among people with disabilities, we all share a labeled defect that overshadows and qualifies many other traits and abilities.

Since stereotypes are often attached to categories of people singled out because of one "negative" attribute in common, those belonging to a category (a minority group) are evaluated on the basis of these stereotypes. Thus, the disabled are assessed by the nondisabled on the bases of the overall stereotype at-

63

tached to their specific disability. And since these stereotypes are usually negative, most of the time the disabled are discriminated against by the nondisabled because the assessment stops at the recognition of the presence of disability.[34]

Frequently the discrimination against people with disabilities diverges from that directed toward other minorities. The prejudice that people with disabilities experience usually takes the more subtle form of pervasive paternalism and social aversion, rather than manifestations of overt bigotry and violence—although in times of economic and social strain violence and bigotry toward people with disabilities become more common. Pervasive paternalism is supported by stereotypes that regard disabilities as signs of weakness, helplessness, and biological inferiority. Aversion is often rooted in people's fears that they or someone about whom they care could become disabled.

Although not all persons with disabilities identify with the disability rights agenda, the existence of an integrated national and international movement of people with disabilities aimed at bettering our position in society indicates a burgeoning sense of group solidarity. This bond, initially formed primarily to respond to the rejection and discrimination of the non-disabled majority, has become one of group pride for the unique dignity and social contributions of people with disabilities. In contrast to dominant stereotypical images of people with disabilities, the shared experience of people with disabilities embodies resourcefulness, independence, and persistence.

Few arguments can be mounted against the contention that people with disabilities involuntarily become members of this minority group. Physical impairments are most often the result of natural causes, such as illnesses, accidents, or genetic conditions, and they become markedly more prevalent with advancing age. All non-disabled people have a certain probability of involuntarily becoming disabled during their lifetimes. However, this probability is not randomly distributed. Studies reveal a disproportionately higher percentage of persons with disabilities among racial minority, elderly, lower socioeconomic, and rural populations. The prevalence of impairment among African Americans is 16.3 percent of the total population, compared with 12.8 percent among whites. Further, the severity of these impairments is greater for African Americans.[35] About twice as many people in families with incomes of less than $20,000 a year are impaired, when compared with the total population. Furthermore, estimates of the percentage of people with disabilities who live in rural areas range from 26 to 33 percent of the total population of the disabled.[36] Thus the likelihood of becoming disabled in our society is closely related to other experiences of social marginalization.

Finally, intermarriage between people with disabilities and the able-bodied is strongly discouraged by societal attitudes. Stereotypic perceptions of people with disabilities as sexually deviant and even dangerous, asexual, or sexually incapacitated owing to physical or emotional impairment severely constrain opportunities for intimate relationships. Research demonstrates that people with disabilities are less likely than non-disabled people to be married, more likely to marry later, and more likely to be divorced.[37] Moreover, while both disabled men and women are perceived as inferior partners, women with disabilities tend to be viewed more negatively by both men and women than comparably disabled men.[38] Given the taboos against intermarriage as well as negative sexual stereotypes of people with disabilities, it is little wonder that people with disabilities are more likely than the non-disabled to be alone.

While the status of people with disabilities as a minority group can be supported, much more research into social structures and relationships that utilizes the minority-group model remains to be done. Examination of the role of environmental segregation in education and employment is crucial to understanding the current status of people with disabilities. More research must be conducted to discover the interrelationship of minority memberships for African American and Hispanic people with disabilities, for example. The inadequacies of the minority-group model refer not to its inability to incorporate the full reality of the experiences of people with disabilities, but to its underuse as a research framework.

Although the number of social scientific studies of disability that refer to people with disabilities as a minority group is increasing, the popular acceptance of this framework and its sociopolitical

65

implications has been tentative and scattered. The perception that disability is a private physical and emotional tragedy to be managed by psychological adjustment, rather than a stigmatized social condition to be redressed through attitudinal changes and social commitment to equality of opportunity for people with disabilities is persistent.

TOWARD A LIBERATORY THEOLOGY: EMPOWERING FRAMEWORKS

The concept of minority group provides a theoretical lens for understanding how such factors as negative stereotypes, prejudice, and discrimination affect the lives of persons with disabilities. Such understanding is the first step toward real communication and ultimately a change in the negative attitudes toward and differential treatment of persons with disabilities. Without a clear acknowledgment that the status of people with disabilities is based on prejudicial attitudes, discrimination, and environmental segregation, no real movement toward emancipatory transformation is possible. The minority-group model gives people with disabilities and those able-bodied individuals and institutions committed to social equality—those others who care—a framework in which to envision change and feasible ideas for bringing it about.

In chapter 2, the alternative knowledge of people with disabilities was revealed in the narratives of two women with disabilities. The real, lived experiences of these women complicated and contradicted stereotypic perceptions of people with disabilities. In chapter 3, the growth of the social movement of people with disabilities and the alternative social scientific paradigms that have accompanied this ascendancy have been chronicled. Though subjected to segregation, stigmatization, and discrimination, people with disabilities have united to initiate social transformation. The body politics of people with disabilities has revealed the hidden history of our bodies in society. We have disclosed the social harm done through segregation and continued marginalization, and we have constructed new models for understanding physical disability.

Yet this movement has been largely ignored by the Christian church. On the whole, denominational support for this social movement has lagged far behind that given to the movements of women and African Americans. In many denominations, discrimination against people with disabilities continues to be condoned. Churches lobbied for and received blanket exemption from the social standards of civil rights instituted by the Americans with Disabilities Act of 1990.[39] Many religious bodies have continued to think of and act as if access for people with disabilities is a matter of benevolence and goodwill, rather than a prerequisite for equality and the foundation on which the church as model of justice must rest. Yet the issue of physical disability has confronted the church perhaps most significantly as a theological challenge.

In chapter 4, I highlight the nature of the theological challenges posed by the individual experiences and social movement of people with disabilities and examine the theological models of disability that have been perpetuated in denominational pronouncements on physical disability. People with disabilities will accept no less than the church's acknowledgment of us as historical actors and theological subjects and its active engagement in eliminating stigmatizing social practices and theological orientations from its midst.

CHAPTER FOUR

CARNAL SINS

As a sacramental community, the Church should signify in its own internal structure the salvation whose fulfillment it announces. Its organization ought to serve this task. As a sign of liberation of humankind and history, the Church itself in its concrete existence ought to be a place of liberation. A sign should be clear and understandable.

Gustavo Gutiérrez[1]

No single story about the relationship between persons with disabilities and the Christian church can express our diverse, complex, and enigmatic connection. This complicated bond underscores the ambiguities of our common life and highlights the tensions in beliefs about trust and suspicion, shame and affirmation, holiness and defilement, sin and grace. Physical disability has served a number of different purposes in Christian history, including, as delineated by one social historian, "to enhance the merits of the just through their patience, to safeguard virtue from pride, to correct the sinner, to proclaim God's glory through miraculous cures and, finally, as the beginning of eternal punishment as in the case of Herod."[2] Clearly, disability has never been religiously neutral, but shot through with theological significance.

Listening for the meanings with which the Christian church has interpreted disability in its midst and has acted toward and with persons with disabilities often uncovers uncertainties and confusions, contradictions and ironies. By sketching the contours of these tangled relations, we may better understand the need for, so to enact, liberatory change and make the church a body of justice for people with disabilities. This chapter starts with our texts, namely, the Bible and theological treatises. Although to my knowledge an extensive examination of biblical interpretation as it regards persons with disabilities has not yet been written and is desperately needed, this chapter does not undertake that project. Instead, the connections between current views and key biblical passages that punctuate the conflicting messages about the theological significance of disability are examined. As a particular case, the theological text of the American Lutheran Church's (ALC) theology of access is scrutinized in the context of the (former) denomination's institutional praxes.[3] The contrast between the ALC's theology of access for persons with disabilities and its policies for ministerial qualification that rejected many persons with disabilities as categorically unsuitable for ordained ministry suggests that too often the outcome of this institutionalized double-minded stance is discrimination and injustice against persons with disabilities.

In the Christian tradition, the acknowledgment of sin is not a shameful thing; rather, it opens a space for the inflowing of grace and acceptance. To be human is to sin; to be a human institution is to institutionalize sin. This chapter, "Carnal Sins," seeks not to vilify individuals or institutions, but rather to make it possible for people with disabilities to struggle for full-bodied participation in God's community and for others who care to cease their conscious and unconscious practices of injustice and turn their energies to doing justice.

DISABLING THEOLOGY

The Christian interpretation of disability has run the gamut from symbolizing sin to representing an occasion for supererogation. The persistent thread within the Christian tradition has been that disability denotes an unusual relationship with God and that the person with disabilities is either divinely blessed or damned: the defiled evildoer or the spiritual superhero. As is often the case with such starkly contrasting characterizations, neither adequately represents the ordinary lives and lived realities of most people with disabilities.

Yet these images can be traced to the biblical record that has shaped our life together as Christians and formed widespread cultural attitudes regarding disability. In the Hebrew Scriptures, in particular, the conflation of moral impurity and physical disability is a common theme. For example, Leviticus 21:17-23 prohibits anyone "blind or lame, or one who has a mutilated face or a limb too long, or one who has a broken foot or a broken hand, or a hunchback, or a dwarf, or a man with a blemish in his eyes" (vv. 18-20) from the priestly activities of bringing offerings to God or entering the most holy place in the temple. These and similar passages have historically been used to warrant barring persons with disabilities from positions of ecclesiastical visibility and authority. The specific physical standards of this passage may not be retained as criteria for today's religious leadership, but the implicit theology that represents disability as being linked with sin, marring the divine image in humans, and preventing religious service persists in church actions and attitudes.

The New Testament also supports this theme of a link between sin and disability. The account of the man with paralysis who was lowered by companions into the house where Jesus was speaking in Luke 5:18-26 has often been interpreted as a story of heroic helpers and a crippled sinner. Here forgiveness of sin and physical healing are represented as equivalent. "Which is easier, to say, 'Your sins are forgiven you,' or to say, 'Stand up and walk'?" (Luke 5:23). John 5:14 recounts the story of the man by the pool of Bethesda. After healing the man, who had been unable to walk, Jesus said, "Do not sin any more, so that nothing worse happens to you." These passages have frequently been cited as proof that disability is a sign of moral imperfection or divine retribution for sin.

John 9:1-3 again represents this sin-disability link, but this time with a different reply from Jesus:

> As [Jesus] walked along, he saw a man blind from birth. His disciples asked him, "Rabbi, who sinned, this man or his parents, that he was born blind?" Jesus answered, "Neither this man nor

71

his parents sinned; he was born blind so that God's works might
be revealed in him."

Thus according to the biblical record, the causal relationship
between sin and impairment is both supported and contradicted
by Jesus. In this passage, Jesus posed an alternative to the commonly accepted notion of cause and effect by interpreting the
man's impairment as an opportunity to manifest the immediacy of
God in an otherwise ordinary life.

Related to the sin-disability conflation is the theme that physical
disability is a travesty of the divine image and an inherent desecra-
tion of all things holy. In the Hebrew Bible and the New Testament,
those who represented God must represent perfection and wholeness (cf. Leviticus 17–26; Heb. 9:14). Theological interpretations
of the meaning of perfection have historically included physical
flawlessness as well as absolute freedom. Both understandings
necessarily exclude the lived realities of people with disabilities (as
well as most other humans). According to such standards, people
with disabilities lack perfection and embody un-wholeness.

The Bible has upheld another theme with respect to people with
disabilities, namely, the ideal of virtuous suffering. The account of
the apostle Paul's "thorn in the flesh," "a messenger of Satan" that
was used by Christ as a sign of divine grace (2 Cor. 12:7-10), has
been influential in supporting a Christian theology of virtuous
suffering. In such passages, righteous submission to divine testing
is upheld as a praiseworthy disposition for Christian disciples.
Likewise, early interpretations of Job and the story of Lazarus
purported that physical impairments were a sign of divine election
by which the righteous were purified and perfected through painful trials. They represent disability as a temporary affliction that
must be endured to gain heavenly rewards.

The biblical support of virtuous suffering has been a subtle, but
particularly dangerous theology for persons with disabilities. Used
to promote adjustment to unjust social situations and to sanction
acceptance of isolation among persons with disabilities, it has
encouraged our passivity and resignation and has institutionalized
depression as an appropriate response to "divine testing." Viewing
suffering as means of purification and of gaining spiritual merit not

only promotes the link between sin and disability but also implies that those who never experience a "cure" continue to harbor sin in their lives. Similar to the practice of emphasizing self-sacrifice to women, the theology of virtuous suffering has encouraged persons with disabilities to acquiesce to social barriers as a sign of obedience to God and to internalize second-class status inside and outside the church.

The biblical theme of charitable giving also has shaped patterns of interaction between able-bodied individuals and those with disabilities. The practice of almsgiving has had equivocal outcomes for marginalized persons, including people with disabilities. In ancient societies, almsgiving provided a vital means of survival for people deemed outcasts or who were without the means to provide for themselves. Yet as the prophet Amos proclaimed, instead of understanding these offerings as the rightful stipends of those who were socially or physically prevented from economic productivity, the people of God pushed aside the needy and refused to establish justice "at the gate" (Amos 5:12-15). Hence, the system of charity that had always included a requirement of justice early failed to accord dignity or even adequate provision.

The obligation to engage in charitable giving is also present in the New Testament. From its inception the Christian community has always acknowledged a special responsibility and mission to marginalized persons, including those who are physically unable to provide for themselves (cf. Acts 6:1-6). Furthermore, several New Testament passages link the notion of charity to healing. For example, in the account of the disabled man at the Beautiful Gate, Peter and John responded to a request for donations with miraculous action. As in this case, often healings restored the person not only to an able-bodied state, but also to social participation and religious inclusion (cf. Acts 3:1-10).

Historically, church-based charitable societies have also merged charity and healing, establishing numerous hospitals and clinics for people with disabilities. The benefits of these organizations should not be underemphasized. They have provided humane care, medical advances, and indispensable financial support. Yet one unintended outcome of the practices of some charitable socie-

73

ties has been the environmental and social segregation of people with disabilities from the Christian community rather than restoration to social and religious participation. Interpreted individualistically, charity and healing result in isolation and alienation from our own nonconventional bodies. Theologian Gustavo Gutiérrez writes:

> It is also necessary to avoid the pitfalls of an individualistic charity. As it has been insisted in recent years, the neighbor is not only a person viewed individually. The term refers also to a person considered in the fabric of social relationships, to a person situated in economic, social, cultural, and racial coordinates. It likewise refers to the exploited class, the dominated people, the marginated.[4]

The themes of individualistic charity and healing neglect the social and political needs of people with disabilities, failing to place as central emphases political engagement and social inclusion. In short, through such actions the Christian church became a prime facilitator of charitable practices that segregated people with disabilities.

These three themes—sin and disability conflation, virtuous suffering, and segregationist charity—illustrate the theological obstacles encountered by people with disabilities who seek inclusion and justice within the Christian community. It cannot be denied that the biblical record and Christian theology have often been dangerous for persons with disabilities. Nor can the prejudice, hostility, and suspicion toward people with disabilities be dismissed as relics of an unenlightened past. Today many interpretations of biblical passages and Christian theologies continue to reinforce negative stereotypes, support social and environmental segregation, and mask the lived realities of people with disabilities. In recent decades, while the problematic nature of the biblical record with regard to women has become generally acknowledged, the degrading depictions of people with disabilities are often ignored, or worse seen as fundamentally accurate to our experience. An uncritical use of the Bible to address the concerns of people with disabilities perpetuates marginalization and discrimination in the name of religion.

In order for the Christian church to stop doing harm and energize their efforts to be a body of justice, critical and careful attention must be given to a theology of disability as an established feature of the systematic theological enterprise. A theology of disability must be made a visible, integral, and ordinary part of the Christian life and our theological reflections on that life. As long as disability is addressed in terms of the themes of sin-disability conflation, virtuous suffering, or charitable action, it will be seen primarily as a fate to be avoided, a tragedy to be explained, or a cause to be championed rather than an ordinary life to be lived. As long as disability is unaddressed theologically or addressed only as a "special interest perspective," the Christian church will continue to propagate a double-minded stance that holds up the disabled as objects of ministry and adulation for overcoming the very barriers that the church has helped to construct. Moreover, the church will squander the considerable theological and practical energies of persons with disabilities who, like other minority groups, call the church to repentance and transformation.

The consequences of relegating a theology of disability to an occasional and peripheral concern can be disastrous not only for people with disabilities, but also for institutional integrity and justice. In the case of the American Lutheran Church, the tragic implication is that even the creation of a theology of access can unintentionally marginalize people with disabilities and open the way for flagrant discrimination.

AN AMERICAN TRAGEDY

In 1980, the General Convention of the American Lutheran Church (ALC) adopted a resolution concerning ministry with persons with disabilities. The resolution was designed to prepare the ALC for the observance in 1981 of the United Nations International Year of the Disabled. Included in the resolution was a theological statement entitled "The Church and Persons with

75

Handicaps: Unmasking a Hidden Curriculum of the Christian Community," a supplementary section entitled "Issues and Implications Evolving from the Theological Statement," and a church school curriculum entitled "An ABC Primer of Faith for the Children of Access." The General Convention ratified the following recommendations: (1) that the divisions and service boards of the ALC, as well as related agencies and institutions, should examine the implications of this statement for their work and reflect the concerns it incorporates; (2) that the ALC should promote the United Nations International Year of the Disabled; (3) that every district of the ALC be encouraged to implement the concerns embodied in this resolution; and (4) that the ALC's office of Communication and Mission Support should study the feasibility of developing programs to address the attitudinal, architectural, and communication barriers that prevent full access by persons with disabilities.[5]

The General Convention of the ALC wholeheartedly embraced the concerns of persons with disabilities and encouraged systemic change. Yet just five years after the unanimous ratification of this resolution, the council of the ALC announced at its 1986 General Convention that people with "significant" physical or mental handicaps would be barred from ordained ministry in the denomination.[6] What had happened?

Despite its broad and well-intentioned goals, the ALC's theology of access and resolution was a non-starter. The institutional change it enjoined did not occur; the issues and implications it raised were affirmed as morally and socially laudable but never satisfactorily incorporated into the church's practices; and the local church education it proposed was not adequately implemented. The denomination that had previously stated "wholeness of the family of God demands not only compassion for the disabled but also their inclusion as fully committed members of the body of Christ who are able to witness and minister,"[7] now asserted that "pastors are expected to be sufficiently able-bodied, ambulatory and mobile" to carry out normal parish duties.[8] Particularly excluded from ministry were persons with neurological disorders such as multiple sclerosis and impairments such as quadriplegia, as well as congenital heart disorders and psychiatric disorders.[9] How could the same body that had ratified a theology of access now block entire categories of people with disabilities from ordained ministry?

Although it would be impossible to identify all the factors that contributed to this ironic and tragic twist, consideration must be given to the likelihood that the direction and content of the ALC's 1980 theology of access itself perpetuated the institutional marginalization of people with disabilities and helped set the stage for the denomination's decision to deny entire groups access to ordained ministry. An exploration of the ALC document's circumstance and substance highlights (1) its problematic stimulus; (2) its neglect of the history of the disability rights movement; (3) the practice of locating able-bodied people at the "speaking center"; (4) its perpetuation of the individual or functional limitation model of disability rather than incorporation of a minority group approach; and (5) a restricted theological focus that fails adequately to address the fundamentals of Lutheran theology, that is, ministry, Word, and Sacraments. These considerations help to place in context the events that occurred in the denomination soon after the adoption of the theology of access.

Another interpretation of the ALC document and the subsequent events might posit that this theology of access at least acknowledged the presence of persons with disabilities in the denomination and educated able-bodied persons about the unique life circumstances of people with disabilities and, therefore, was better than nothing at all. Such an assessment, however, discounts the potency of institutional discrimination and the means by which its segregationist practices gain legitimacy. It capitulates before the document's conception of disability as a solely individual characteristic that fosters institutional practices which categorize and discriminate on the basis of impairment. It fails to account for the burdensome quality of an ostensibly liberating discourse that occupies our time with the perpetual instruction of the able-bodied rather than our own liberation. In its neglect of the history of disability activism, it fails to recognize people with disabilities as historical actors.

77

Although identifying the specific factors that motivate any institution to engage in theological reflection is exceedingly difficult, in the case of the ALC theology of access, the document includes a statement that highlights its decision to address the status of people with disabilities in the denomination in accordance with the United Nations upcoming "Year for the Disabled," as 1981 was designated. The history of that UN event is thus particularly instructive.

The preparations for the UN program were fraught with discord because of the organization's failure to confer with activists and groups of people with disabilities. The initial designation "Year for the Disabled" was changed to the "International Year of Disabled People" only after considerable lobbying by activists who protested that the "Year for" title implied passivity and perpetuated inadequate models of charitable assistance.[10] The World Program of Action Concerning Disabled People formulated in preparation for 1981 also was eventually redrafted, because it initially emphasized the functional limitation model of disability and failed to build in continuing consultation with organizations of people with disabilities.[11] Preparations for the Year of Disabled People revealed to UN officials the new dynamics that were emerging among people with disabilities. Increasingly people with disabilities were willing to cooperate with such "Year of" projects only if they were involved in establishing the agenda and conceptual framework. Eventually UN organizations acknowledged that persons with disabilities as citizens

> have the right to participate fully in society and utilize community service[s] the same as every other citizen. Thus the World Program of Action is based on the principles of human rights, full participation, self-determination, integration into society and equalization of opportunity, while the traditional model was based on segregation, institutionalization, and professional control.[12]

The experience of the UN anticipates the predicament of the ALC's theology of access. The denomination evidently responded to the UN call for action without learning from the UN's missteps, including the need for early consultation with a variety of individuals and groups of people with disabilities. In responding to the call from our international social conscience directed primarily to powerful institutions, the ALC perpetuated the hierarchical approach promulgated by the United Nations. In defining the need for a theology of access, the denomination identified a professional to draft a statement without early engagement with organizations of people with disabilities inside and outside the denomination.

Furthermore, the ALC failed to anticipate the possibility that the UN's "Year of" approach could foster cyclical consideration of the continuing problem of the marginalization of and discrimination against people with disabilities. Social critic Leslie Fiedler has identified this pitfall inherent in the UN approach and in those that follow its lead.

> Recently the adult 'normals,' chiefly male, who make such decisions for the United Nations have decreed that each three hundred and sixty-five days we live be dedicated to one or another of the sub-groups in society in relation to whom they feel most deeply conflicted—most guiltily aware of a discrepancy between their avowed attitudes and covert prejudices. We have had in succession, therefore, the Year of the Woman, the Year of the Child and finally the Year of the Disabled.[13]

Fiedler not only highlights the transience of the "Year of" approach, but underscores the power differential that enables certain individuals and groups to make other groups and individuals the "topic" of the year. People with disabilities are particularly cognizant of this dynamic of becoming the annual "topic" since for decades in the United States, people with disabilities have been depicted in annual television telethons as objects of pity or courage, desperate for aid. These events tend to perpetuate able-bodied people's stereotypes of the lives of individuals with disabilities and often fund agencies in which people with disabilities have relatively little power or voice. By making of people with disabilities a "topic" to be examined instead of seeing them as ordinary people who need access to positions of power, these events or pronouncements tend to defend the balance of power that must be overcome if

79

lasting change is to be engendered. Advocacy begun by powerful institutions at the behest of other powerful institutions without early and enduring consultation with people with disabilities is particularly at risk of failing its marginalized constituency.

Instead of promoting dialogue among persons with disabilities whereby issues of vital concern could be addressed or speaking to persons with disabilities about their experience in the denomination, the American Lutheran Church began by addressing the "topic" of persons with disabilities in their theology of access. This approach, in contrast to one that would initiate public meetings among people with disabilities or seek direction from existing disability organizations, failed to locate people with diverse disabilities at the center of power and to engage organizations that serve their self-identified needs.

Second, the ALC document does not connect its effort with the continuing struggle for justice by the disability rights movement. The disability rights movement's struggle for justice and social inclusion had been underway since the 1960s, yet nowhere in the document is its existence mentioned. In fact, when the passage of the Rehabilitation Act of 1973 (Section 504) is noted in the document, HEW Secretary Joseph Califano is presented as an advocate for persons with disabilities. In fact, in 1977, four years after its passage, Califano still refused to sign regulations implementing Section 504. In San Francisco, activists in the disability rights movement occupied the HEW offices for twenty-eight days until the regulations were signed.[14] This event was a watershed incident in the history of the disability rights movement. The increased awareness of people with disabilities that could prompt an International Year of the Disabled or a denomination-wide theology of access was an outgrowth of the activism of the disability rights movement. Yet nowhere in the document was this vital struggle credited.

Although the document does not recount the hard-won successes of the disability rights movement, it does acknowledge its impact by making an underhanded attack on the movement's tactics as unchristian. "Every Christian, therefore, is a 'dis-enabled' person. When this is taught, militant activity will not be necessary.

Militancy is a threat to unity because it overemphasizes the 'we' and 'they' dichotomy."[15] The document disregards the accomplishments of the disability rights movement, opting instead to express disapproval of the strategies that have oftentimes produced policy changes and awareness of the rightful claims of people with disabilities.

Unity is, of course, a worthwhile goal, but a unity that silences the call of marginalized people for justice is not true unity. Real unity can come only by difficult truth-telling and open discussion of the discrimination experienced by many people with disabilities. Unity must be predicated upon justice. By failing to stand in solidarity with those who are already working for liberation, the ALC theology of access reveals that an acquiescent unity rather than resolute solidarity is the document's aim. Advancement of the cause of any marginalized group cannot be achieved by neglecting the history of the struggle against discrimination and injustice. A theology that fails to come to terms with the catalysts for resistance and those circumstances necessary to sustain it in specific, historical situations cannot fully comprehend the insidious character of discrimination and the persistence critical to seeking justice.

This failure to acknowledge the debt to disability activists is linked to the document's failure to locate people with disabilities at the "speaking center."[16] Many persons with disabilities have yet to experience being at the speaking center—not only talking about ourselves but talking to other people with disabilities. Generally we struggle to explain our experiences in terms that able-bodied persons can grasp. Yet this act of translation, when unaccompanied by routine experiences of talking and listening to other people with disabilities, can distort and limit our understanding. We can fail to give voice to those experiences outside the knowledge of our able-bodied interlocutors. bell hooks, describing these dynamics, writes:

> If the identified audience, those spoken to, is determined solely by ruling groups who control production and distribution, then it is easy for the marginal voice striving for a hearing to allow what is said to be overdetermined by the needs of that majority group who appear to be listening, to be tuned in. It becomes

81

easy to speak about what that group wants to hear, to describe and define experience in a language compatible with existing images and ways of knowing, constructed within the social frameworks that reinforce domination.[17]

The practice of locating people with disabilities at the speaking center necessitates a community identification. Unlike some other minority groups, for example, African Americans and Jews, people with disabilities often lack the familial and social experiences that facilitate this awareness. The history of people with disabilities is frequently absent from school curricula. Children with disabilities are seldom taught by disabled adults to be proud of the characteristics valued in the community of people with disabilities but devalued in the dominant society.

Not surprisingly, the disability rights movement emerged in those settings where people with disabilities could talk to one another. This liberatory dialogue enabled marginalized people to uncover the danger in assimilating mainstream values about their lives and bodies and enabled them to link their experiences to those of others. Understanding individual experiences in terms of a community or group makes possible the move from object to subject and the liberatory voice, that is, "a way of speaking that is no longer determined by one's status as object."[18] Facilitating this type of community identification and awareness is the first step toward empowerment.

In the ALC theology of access, the able-bodied church is at the speaking center. Persons with disabilities are the topic. The document addresses itself to the able-bodied church, urging it to promote the needs of persons with disabilities, rather than speaking directly to persons with disabilities within the denomination, empowering them to claim their voice and to assert their demands for justice. The document features what the able-bodied church thinks it knows about persons with disabilities and how that differs from what it actually practices. Even on the level of semantics, persons with disabilities become third-person objects, and the able-bodied church becomes the first-person subject. For example:

As a community of faith that responds to God's healing work in Christ, the church is now challenged at least to assist in implementing the leadership of secular authorities in this case. . . . The presence of the handicapped among us reminds us of the fragility of human life.[19]

Any theology that seeks access for people with disabilities must necessarily come from a liberatory voice that continues to be constituted by a dialogue within the community of people with disabilities that locates us at the speaking center. It must recognize itself as participating in a group's "permanent effort . . . to situate themselves in time and space, to exercise their creative potential, and to assume their responsibilities."[20] It must come from the perspective of persons with disabilities and address other people with disabilities as the center of its concern. Likewise, it must appreciate the diversity within this community and its ever-changing character.

Dialogue and study among people with disabilities have resulted in an alternative framework for understanding disability, namely, the minority-group model, addressed in chapter 3. Yet the ALC document does not engage this model. Defining people with disabilities as individuals "whose difficulties are sufficiently severe to set them apart from the norm or ordinary ways of living, learning and doing things," the document perpetuates an individual or functional limitation approach to disability.[21] As already noted, the individual or functional limitations model focuses on the private physical impairments and identifies psychological adjustment as the primary rehabilitative goal. It discounts architectural and attitudinal barriers as the primary cause of marginalization among people with disabilities.

Building its theological perspectives on the functional limitation model, the ALC document adds theological justification to this approach's emphasis on adjustment. David Tracy's "concept of limits" in *Blessed Rage for Order* is used to constitute a theology of disability that posits submission and adjustment as its primary aims. The goal of "total indifference to one's disability" while seen as an elusive ideal is replaced by "internaliz[ing] the limit situation and decid[ing] to cope with a personal predicament."[22] The theology

83

contends that the individual with a disability must develop strategies to compensate for her or his disability in a society that is hostile toward that person. She or he must "acknowledge an erosion of spirit" caused by disability and recognize that "physical wholeness will never be known or achieved again."[23] Not surprisingly, the document addresses the pervasive depression experienced by persons with disabilities as an element of our functional limitations, rather than a response to the social isolation we experience.

The document's individualistic approach to disability resulted in an individualistic theology. The ALC document proposes a theological interpretation of disability understood in terms of limitation and defect. The concept of limit, as proposed by Tracy, is intended primarily for those who live in abundance and whose consumerist practices defy the reality of global scarcity. To interpret this theological concept as a call to people with disabilities to internalize limit situations fails to distinguish audiences and approximates preaching poverty to the poor. Clearly disabilities place limits on individuals. So too does ordinary life place limits on people. The distinguishing social factor with regard to people with disabilities is that society places many additional limits upon us.

Furthermore, the social limits we face are not adequately resisted by deciding, as the ALC document suggests, "to choose one's attitude in any given set of circumstances, to choose one's own way."[24] For people who are keenly and painfully aware of their suffering from injustice and marginalization, to advocate primarily individualistic prescriptions leads to despair and powerlessness. Proposing primarily individualistic solutions to worldwide social injustice, the document fails to observe among many people with disabilities a desire for liberatory action and a movement of struggle for justice, not only to obtain limited access to existing structures and systems of power, but also to uncover the hidden history of people with disabilities, to transform existing structures, to identify ourselves as theological subjects, and to express the theological symbols that show the lived realities of our lives.

The limited scope of the ALC theology of access is further revealed in its focus on only two arenas of theological discourse, pastoral care and Christian education. The document primarily addresses the need for new models of pastoral care "with" persons with disabilities rather than "for" us, and Christian education that is purged of the hidden agenda of discrimination toward people with disabilities. The document proposes education accomplished by analogy. The able-bodied person must be taught that the person with disabilities is almost the same as him or her. One argument follows:

> A Christian education devoted to the "deliberate and intentional attending in the present to the future possibility of the total person and the Christian community" is a place to begin. . . . We will learn together that only God himself is able and that each of us is disabled by the Fall. But in Christ God sets us free and enables us to do his will. Every Christian, therefore, is a "dis-enabled" person.[25]

By spiritualizing disability to argue that all Christians are disabled by sin and are, therefore, "dis-enabled," the document obscures the concrete reality of the exclusion of people with disabilities from participation in the Christian community. While all people do experience sin, not all people face architectural segregation and discrimination on the basis of disability.

Education as analogy also means that we are locked into the able-bodied categories of reality. Persons with disabilities can suggest alterations that would make sense according to the preexistent order of things, but we cannot engage in transformative discourses and resymbolization. By failing to assert the importance of disabled persons' self-understandings and specific knowledges for revisioning the theological foundations of ministry, Word and Sacraments, the document calls for inclusion on the terms set down by able-bodied persons, rather than for transformation of those theological and institutional foundations that would enable the inclusion of people with disabilities. This becomes particularly evident in the document's advocacy of a classification system for stipulating "degrees of handicapping disabilities for ordained and public ministries"[26] because of the distraction and congregational discomfort caused by persons with visible disabilities and dictated by the level of impairment that can be tolerated without substantively changing religious rituals. Asserting that persons with disabilities should consider lay rather than clergy positions of ministry, the document poses the question "Will 'lay' ministry among the disabled become the better option for the future?"[27] These propositions prefigured the institutional practice of discrimination adopted by the General Convention in 1986.

The ALC's theology of access was fundamentally flawed and actually nurtured stigmatization that became sanctified by denominational polity in 1986. The conception and the content of its theology of access unwittingly legitimated the segregation and exclusion of some people with disabilities while ostensibly advocating change. By denying some people with disabilities even the possibility of ordained ministry, the American Lutheran Church ignored the distinct gifts and graces of entire categories of ministerial candidates and abrogated their institutional usefulness on the basis of their nonconventional bodies. Failing to heed James's warning against being "double-minded" (1:8 and 4:8), the denomination spoke one way and acted another.

LIBERATING COMMITMENT AND CONSISTENCY

For people with disabilities, a liberatory theology draws together message and commitment. It acknowledges our struggle against the discrimination that is pervasive within the church and society as a part of the work of coming to our bodies. A liberatory theology sustains our difficult but ordinary lives, empowers and collaborates with individuals and groups of people with disabilities who struggle for justice in concrete situations, creates new ways of resisting the theological symbols that exclude and devalue us, and reclaims our hidden history in the presence of God on earth.

Before revisioning can occur, we must perceive clearly the consequences of relegating theology of disability to an occasional and peripheral concern. In this chapter, I began the reclamation process by identifying the specific dangers and practices of institutional double-mindedness. By recounting the particular history of discrimination within the American Lutheran Church, I sketched necessary components of a liberatory theology. A liberatory theology of disability comes from the perspective of persons with disabilities and addresses other people with disabilities as the center of its concern. By declaring the possibility of justice and generating resistance in specific, historical situations, it helps foster community awareness and connects its theological reflection to the communities of persons with disabilities who are already mobilized in the struggle for justice. A liberatory theology of disability is liberating from its inception, incorporating dialogical rather than hierarchical relations. It represents the permanent effort of persons with disabilities to incorporate ourselves in time and space, to exercise our creative capacity, and to assume our responsibilities within the church. It begins with the understanding that people with disabilities, rather than being individuals who cannot measure up to the normal practices of society, constitute a disadvantaged minority group. It stigmatizes particular institutions and social attitudes, rather than our nonconventional bodies. It calls the church to embody justice as its fundamental mission. A liberatory theology of disability critically engages the fundamental theologies of the Christian tradition.

In chapter 5, I explore the revolutionary implications of the resurrected Christ as the disabled God, a divine affirmation of the wholeness of nonconventional bodies. Liberatory themes are latent within the biblical record, namely, the image of the disabled God and the affirmation of the full participation of persons with disabilities in the community of faith that makes possible corporate healing and new models of wholeness. If the real, lived experiences of people with disabilities are to be recognized, then Christ's disabled body must be acknowledged as part of the Christian legacy, and its celebration in the Eucharist must become a symbol of an altered vision of spiritual and physical reconciliation and wholeness. The centrality of the Eucharist in the symbolic and actual inclusion of people with disabilities is the central focus of chapter 6.

CHAPTER FIVE

THE DISABLED GOD

We have seen signs which shall not be cut off. The branches shall not be cut off from the vine. Our power will not be diminished or rendered ineffective. The sacrament of life shall not be withheld—the body, the blood, the sensuality of God's presence on earth.

Carter Heyward[1]

For me, epiphanies come too infrequently to be shrugged off as unbelievable. Like a faithful Jew who had conscientiously opened the door for Elijah each Seder and spun images of the majestic beauty of a Messiah who would shout out an order and the universe would tremble, I had waited for a mighty revelation of God. But my epiphany bore little resemblance to the God I was expecting or the God of my dreams. I saw God in a sip-puff wheelchair, that is, the chair used mostly by quadriplegics enabling them to maneuver by blowing and sucking on a strawlike device. Not an omnipotent, self-sufficient God, but neither a pitiable, suffering servant. In this moment, I beheld God as a survivor, unpitying and forthright. I recognized the incarnate Christ in the image of those judged "not feasible," "unemployable," with "questionable quality of life." Here was God for me.

After glimpsing this hidden image of God, I began to think and to share my contemplations with friends in the disability rights movement. Making sense of our fascination with and appreciation of that image has been a driving force for this book. This theology of liberation emerged from those conversations, our common labor for justice, and corporate reflection on symbol. Although this work cannot represent the experience of all people with disabilities

89

who seek justice and God with equal fervor, it is a beginning and an invitation to emancipatory transformation for both people with disabilities and others who care. By beginning with the experience of persons with disabilities, recounting our history of the disability rights movement, examining models for understanding disability, and naming the injustice wrought in the name of Christian good-will, I have engaged in the theological task of describing as accurately as possible how things are for people with disabilities. Yet the method used here attempts not only to unmask our real, lived experience, making our multifaceted body knowledge a resource for "doing theology," but also to offer a vision of a God who is for us and a church that is for that God and persons with disabilities as the people of God.

In this chapter, I explore a liberatory theology of disability that incorporates both political action and reconception of symbols. Emancipatory transformation must be enacted not only in history, but also in imagination and language. Liberatory theology of disability is the work of the bodily figuration of knowledge.[2] As embodied theology, it is both the struggle of resistance and the revelation of our long-masked knowledge and images. It is not an abstract theory, but is grounded in the bodies and actions of people with disabilities and others who care. To speak of a liberatory proclamation for people with disabilities is to recognize, as Nancy Mairs maintains, that a voice is the creature of the body that produces it. A liberatory theology of disability begins with our bodies and keeps faith with our hidden history. This liberatory theology recognizes biblical revelation and truth in those texts and interpretative models that transcend their able-bodied frameworks—which isolate and stigmatize people with disabilities—and that permit a vision of people with disabilities as theological subjects and historical actors. One locus of such revelation and truth is embodied in the image of Jesus Christ, the disabled God.

ON INCARNATING LIBERATION

In exploring the relationship between physical embodiment and religious symbols, two fundamental insights must be acknowledged. First, all human beings are embodied. Feminists have directed our attention to the gender of those bodies as fundamental to our understanding of religious experience. They note that the experiences of men and women are seldom the same socially or religiously. People with disabilities have contended that embodiment includes physical ability as well. By focusing on the physical status of individuals, people with disabilities have questioned the use of "normal" bodies as the basis for scholarly study of religion or practice of religious ritual.

Second, religious symbols point individuals beyond their ordinary lives. Religious symbols not only prescribe or reproduce social status, but they also transform it. The power of symbols and myths is in the motive force they engender. Clifford Geertz, an anthropologist, maintains that symbols have performative power for societies and individuals because they establish and maintain beliefs and values—a cultural ethos. "Religion is a system of symbols which acts to produce powerful, pervasive, and long-lasting moods and motivations in [people] by formulating conceptions of a general order of existence."[3] By "moods," Geertz means psychological dispositions, such as self-confidence, awe, or trust. "Motivation" is the tendency to act or feel a particular way. Symbols create normative standards for human interaction. They legitimate social structures, political arrangements, and attitudinal inclinations, constitute our cultural toolkits, and offer visions of what can be. Carol Christ argues that it is because of this performative power that oppressive symbol systems cannot simply be repudiated, but must be replaced. She writes, "Where there is not any replacement, the mind will revert to familiar structures at times of crises, bafflement, or defeat."[4]

Empowering symbols are vital for any marginalized group. Yet if thoroughgoing transformation is the aim, those reconceived symbols must be linked to the dominant social-symbolic order. That is, not only must they change the way that people with disabilities conceive of our experiences and, in particular, our relationships to God, they must also alter the regular practices, ideas, and images of the able-bodied. The obstacles that confront us in our daily lives are held in place by the images, ideas, and

91

emotional responses of an able-bodied society. Hence a separatist symbol system for people with disabilities would perpetuate the segregation that is already too often our practical reality. Furthermore, separatism would deny our real interdependence with able-bodied persons. We need symbols that affirm our dignity in relation not only to other people with disabilities, but also to able-bodied persons. We need symbols that call both people with disabilities and the able-bodied to conversion.

My focus on symbols as crucial for emancipatory transformation is a strategic judgment about the power of religious symbols with reference to disability. The importance of visibility in the stigmatization of people with disabilities and discourse about disability, suggests that a liberatory theology of disability must create new images of wholeness as well as new discourses. Furthermore, the bodily rituals of stigmatization and exclusion that are a significant form of oppression of people with disabilities must be supplanted by bodily practices of ordinary inclusion.

The stigmatization of people with disabilities is not simply a matter of rationalized and deliberate institutional and individual discrimination, though it is unquestionably that; it is also a condition of the modern human psyche and a physical stance of being. Iris Marion Young states,

> Group oppressions are enacted in this society not primarily in official laws and policies but in informal, often unnoticed and unreflective speech, bodily reactions to others, conventional practices of everyday interactions and evaluations, aesthetic judgments, and the jokes, images, and stereotypes pervading the mass media.[5]

For people with disabilities, the bodily reactions of the able-bodied are often particularly oppressive. Goffman calls them rituals of degradation.[6] For example, people who use wheelchairs endure physical debasement when people refuse to meet their eyes or stand beside the chair to talk instead of before the person. Deep-seated unconscious aversion to people with disabilities is typically enacted and upheld by attitudinal barriers and physical avoidance. Stigmatization sometimes also takes the form of inappropriate fascination with the bodies of people with disabilities. Often strangers in elevators ask me what I did to myself. This inappropriate curiosity, defended as charitable goodwill, is a ritual enactment of patterns of social power in which able-bodied people assume an exceptional access to the bodies of people with disabilities.

As asserted in chapter 4, these attitudinal barriers are funded by foundational Christian themes such as the conflation of sin and disability, virtuous suffering, and segregationist charity. The social-symbolic order that these Christian theologies help to establish perpetuates the belief that disability is inherently "un(w)holy" and that the suffering of people with disabilities is the natural outcome of our impairments. Institutional practices also dissipate our yearning for justice, substituting instead self-pity and the isolating charity of others. These Christian theologies defraud people with disabilities by undercutting our self-empowerment and frustrating our liberatory work. They sometimes seduce people with disabilities into sharing the prejudices about ourselves and others held by the able-bodied community, leading to feelings of self-rejection and shame. The symbols also promote the mood and motivation of charity, which sanctions dependency as an appropriate Christian virtue.

The most promising model for addressing this real institutional discrimination and submerged cultural imperialism, that is, "the universalization of a dominant group's experience and culture, and its establishment as the norm,"[7] is through a liberatory theology of disability that includes both political action and resymbolization. Emancipatory transformation must include not only an examination of dominant practices and beliefs and the ways in which they maintain or challenge structures of stigmatization and marginalization, but also a search for and proclamation of alternative structures and symbols of religious life that can effectively challenge oppressive beliefs and values. Rebecca S. Chopp writes:

> Until we change the values and hidden rules that run through present linguistic practices, social codes, and psychic orderings, women, persons of color, and other oppressed groups will be forced—by language, discourses, and practices available to

93

them—into conforming to ongoing practices, to babbling nonsense, or to not speaking at all.[8]

In changing the symbol of Christ, from that of suffering servant, model of virtuous suffering, or conquering lord, toward a formulation of Jesus Christ as disabled God, I draw implications for the ritual and doctrine of the Eucharist based on this new symbol. This two-step theological construction intends constitutive change and the creation of new symbols and rituals whereby people with disabilities can affirm our bodies in dignity and reconceive the church as community of justice for people with disabilities. Thus the truth of these theological statements is in their ability to transform reality, not necessarily for all people at all times, but for particular people in particular situations of oppression and pain. The truth of this liberatory theology of disability is in its ability to enable transformation for people with disabilities within the church and in its adaptability to addressing our ever-emerging challenges and opportunities. In order to accomplish these goals, the thoroughgoing transformation of institutional, bureaucratic, and theological foundations of the Christian church is essential.

ACTING OUT AND HOLDING OUR BODIES TOGETHER

This theological method joins political action and resymbolization. Political action is the work of "acting out" and "holding our bodies together" in the struggle against the overt discrimination endemic in society and the church. Political action includes increasing the visibility and authority of people with disabilities, promoting face-to-face interaction between people with disabilities and the able-bodied, and emphasizing the communal benefit afforded by the inclusion of a minority viewpoint. These activities question and disrupt able-bodied society's stance toward people with disabilities. As Iris Marion Young asserts, "Encounter with the disabled person again produces the ambiguity of recognizing that the person whom I project as so different, so other, is nevertheless like me."[9] "Acting out" means refusing to acquiesce to the acceptable role for people with disabilities; it is the revolutionary work of resistance. "Holding our bodies together" is the work of solidarity with our own bodies, other people with disabilities, and other marginalized groups.

Acting out involves being willing to expend our sometimes flagging store of energy on the struggle for justice. It is risking acknowledgment of how weary we are of oppression. Fatigue is a double-edged sword for people with disabilities. Often our bone-weariness with living a difficult life made more difficult by stigmatizing social systems necessitates that we rebel. Yet people with disabilities cannot afford to ignore or underestimate the real work of liberation. We must and have learned to pick our battles carefully. Though we do not necessarily opt only for winnable campaigns, we must always be aware of the implications of any one struggle for advancing our common cause.

Fatigue can also cut us off from our corporate energy. We must tend to our families and friends and generate the requisite quantity and quality of labor at our jobs, as well as put our bodies on American Disabled for Attendant Programs Today (ADAPT) protest lines, write letters to legislators, organize ourselves, and attend our meetings. Hence actual liberation requires that our liberatory practices incorporate our need for health and survival. Displacing the notion of virtuous suffering from the church, only to reinstitute it as revolutionary practice is not emancipatory for people with disabilities. Our physical and communal survival requires that a first-order priority of a liberatory theology is the creation of positions that enable people to work full-time for liberation within the disability community and within the church.

Second, acting out and holding our bodies together requires coming to terms with our own bodies—bodies that sometimes throw us to the pavement simply for placing our feet carelessly, and bodies that twitch and pitch, searching for an ever-elusive comfortable position. Embodiment is not a purely agreeable reality; it incorporates profound ambiguity—sometimes downright distress. There is simply no denying it. We concede the precarious position of living a difficult life and affirming our bodies as whole, good,

95

and beautiful. In this incongruity, the revolutionary act of accepting our bodies as "survive-able," not deficient or deformed, is vital. "Survive-able" bodies are painstakingly, honestly, and lovingly constructed, not, according to Nancy Mairs, "heroic figure[s], wounded but still defiant."[10] Instead of flagellating ourselves or aspiring to well-behaved "perfect" bodies, we savor the jumbled pleasure-pain that is our bodies. In a society where denial of our particular bodies and questing for a better body is "normal," respect for our own bodies is an act of resistance and liberation.

Further, holding our bodies together denotes attention to our sexuality as a resource for solidarity with one another and with ourselves. We maintain that knowledge is fundamentally relational. Hence it is dynamic, rather than static. Audre Lorde attends to this notion of the body as erotic.

> The erotic . . . provides the power which comes from sharing deeply any pursuit with another person. The sharing of joy, whether physical, emotional, psychic, or intellectual, forms a bridge between the sharers which can be the basis for understanding much of what is not shared between them, and lessens the threat of their difference.[11]

This erotic understanding is revealed in Diane DeVries's description of her relation with her sister and her embodiment of Debbie's body. The power of this interconnection is its genesis in shared bodies and lives and its synergistic pleasure. Among people with disabilities, holding our bodies together touches the "joy we know ourselves to be capable of"[12] and emerges from a complex and concrete love of life. This erotic power draws us out of our physical isolation; it is the "laying on of hands" that releases the embodied power of God on earth.

Holding our bodies together also means placing ourselves in solidarity with other people with disabilities. It means not distinguishing between "good" and "bad" disabilities, refusing to stigmatize people with intellectual disabilities as inherently more impaired than those with ambulatory disabilities, for example. For those very few "token" individuals who are allowed to succeed in the able-bodied system, it means refusing to be flattered into believing that our "extraordinary" achievements are the result of our atypical intelligence and talent. By holding our bodies together, we turn our backs on a social system that institutionalizes horizontal violence as the toll charge of inclusion.

Finally, holding our bodies together means uniting with other marginalized peoples in resistance. A liberatory theology of disability is in solidarity with other liberation theologies, though it incorporates unique emphases and perspectives. Structures and attitudes that keep women, people of color, and the poor marginalized also stigmatize people with disabilities as their "normal" practice. Hence the consciousness-raising efforts of other marginalized people have provided both motivation and models for people with disabilities. A liberatory theology of disability shares with feminist theology a valuation of the body as a theological resource. It, too, challenges the patriarchal image of God. Following Latin American liberation theologians, a liberatory theology of disability calls for justice for the poor. Only institutionalized violence and systemic torture can explain why malnutrition is the primary cause of disability worldwide. It is estimated that there are at least 600 million people worldwide who have disabilities. Malnutrition accounts for approximately 20 percent of that disablement.[13] Bearing witness for peace and struggling against the weapons trade, a liberatory theology of disability calls for an end to the violence which tears at bodies and multiplies refugees, who often suffer undernourishment and inadequate care for injuries. With those who resist not-so-subtle racism in educational practices that conceal potent resistance narratives, a theology of disability seeks to uncover and expound the history of resistance to oppression.

Although acting out and holding our bodies together are essential liberatory tactics, they are not enough. While I hope with Pat Wright, once director of the Disability Rights Education and Defense Fund, who writes, "You can't legislate attitudes, but the attitudinal barriers will drop the more disabled people are employed, the more they can be seen on the street and when we become not just a silent minority, but fully participating members of society,"[14] I am less confident that the presence of our bodies in

97

public will displace the pervasive belief structure that thrives on our subjugation. As the history of the disability rights movement demonstrates and as marginalized people already know, political action does not thoroughly alter the attitudes that underlie discrimination. A liberatory theology of disability must also incorporate resymbolization aimed at these attitudinal supports. It must create new symbols of wholeness and new embodiments of justice.

Resymbolization entails the deconstruction of dominant symbolic meanings and a reconstitution of those symbols, making them both liberatory for the marginalized group and unsettling for the dominant group. Resymbolization is radical symbol sedition. Following Paul Ricoeur's proposition that the symbol gives rise to thought, I maintain that the symbol can also give rise to subversive thought and action.[15] A symbol can be reclaimed as part of a hidden history. It is this decentering of the dominant symbolic order that resists "normal" attitudes and unconscious prejudice. It is this paradoxical coexistence of difference and sameness incorporated into familiar symbols that infiltrates the misleading mystifications of disability and demythologizes the mythic archetypes of suffering and heroic survival. Although this process recognizes that people with disabilities are not at home within the Christian tradition and the social-symbolic order it has engendered, it suggests that we are not as estranged as the able-bodied church and society portrays us. We have been hidden, but we haven't gone away. Our hidden history is latent within the Christian symbols, and we will not be cut off.

THE DISABLED GOD

A reconception of the symbol of Jesus Christ, as disabled God, is developed here as a contextualized Christology. It is contextualized in that the disabled God emerges in the particular situation in which people with disabilities and others who care find themselves as they try to live out their faith and to fulfill their calling to live ordinary lives of worth and dignity. Contextualization is an authentic process of perceiving how God is present with people with

98

disabilities and of unmasking the ways in which theological inquiry has frequently instituted able-bodied experience as the theological norm. The theological lenses through which we have traditionally viewed our own and others' bodies distort the physical presence not only of people with disabilities but also of the incarnate God. To contextualize then is both to engage the past and present of a biblical text or a religious symbol in light of the past and present of its readers and hearers and to look to the future and the transformative effect that such a reading can have upon those who will come into contact with it.

Christology is the natural domain of contextualization since the Incarnation is the ultimate contextual revelation. Orlando E. Costas writes, "Biblical contextualization is rooted in the fact that the God of revelation can only be known in history. Such a revelation comes to specific peoples in concrete situations by means of particular cultural symbols and categories."[16] God became flesh in a particular time and place. Through centuries of theological abstractions, the power of that very physical reality of God present in human flesh has sometimes been obscured. Yet Christology is fundamentally about human experience and human bodies as partially constitutive of God. God is with us: Emmanuel (Matt. 1:22-23). As Nancy Mairs writes:

A God who put on a body and walked about in that body and spoke to us from that body and died as that body and yet somehow did not die then or ever but lives on in our bodies which live in God. It's not the easiest story to swallow.[17]

The coming of Emmanuel was understood by the early church in terms of the death and resurrection.[18] At the resurrection, the disciples understood the person Jesus for who he really was. Only through the lens of resurrection could they understand the meaning and significance of the life of Jesus on earth. In the resurrected Jesus Christ, they saw not the suffering servant for whom the last and most important word was tragedy and sin, but the disabled God who embodied both impaired hands and feet and pierced side and the imago Dei. Paradoxically, in the very act commonly understood as the transcendence of physical life, God is revealed as tangible,

99

bearing the representation of the body reshaped by injustice and sin into the fullness of the Godhead. Luke 24:36-39 relates an appearance of this resurrected Jesus:

> While they were talking about this, Jesus himself stood among them. . . . They were startled and terrified, and thought that they were seeing a ghost. He said to them, "Why are you frightened, and why do doubts arise in your hearts? Look at my hands and my feet; see that it is I myself. Touch me and see; for a ghost does not have flesh and bones as you see that I have."

Here is the resurrected Christ making good on the incarnational proclamation that God would be with us, embodied as we are, incorporating the fullness of human contingency and ordinary life into God. In presenting his impaired hands and feet to his startled friends, the resurrected Jesus is revealed as the disabled God. Jesus, the resurrected Savior, calls for his frightened companions to recognize in the marks of impairment their own connection with God, their own salvation. In so doing, this disabled God is also the revealer of a new humanity. The disabled God is not only the One from heaven but the revelation of true personhood, underscoring the reality that full personhood is fully compatible with the experience of disability.

THEOLOGICAL IMPLICATIONS OF THE DISABLED GOD

The symbol of Jesus Christ, the disabled God, has transformative power. It is the experience of Christ from below as a corporeal experience. The power of the disabled God is the seemingly inherent contradiction this God embodies. This revelation of God disorders the social-symbolic order, and God appears in the most unexpected bodies. The disabled God does not engage in a battle for dominance or create a new normative power, God is in the present social-symbolic order at the margins with people with disabilities and instigates transformation from this de-centered position.

The disabled God repudiates the conception of disability as a consequence of individual sin. Injustice against persons with disabilities is surely sin; our bodies, however, are not artifacts of sin, original or otherwise. Our bodies participate in the imago Dei, not in spite of our impairments and contingencies, but through them. The conflation of sin and disability causes problems for the interpretation of the resurrected Jesus Christ. What is the significance of the resurrected Christ's display of impaired hands and feet and side? Are they the disfiguring vestiges of sin? Are they to be subsumed under the image of Christ, death conqueror? Or should the disability of Christ be understood as the truth of incarnation and the promise of resurrection? The latter interpretation fosters a reconception of wholeness. It suggests a human-God who not only knows injustice and experiences the contingency of human life, but also reconceives perfection as unself-pitying, painstaking survival.

The resurrected Jesus Christ in presenting impaired hands and feet and side to be touched by frightened friends alters the taboo of physical avoidance of disability and calls for followers to recognize their connection and equality at the point of Christ's physical impairment. Christ's disfigured side bears witness to the existence of "hidden" disabilities, as well. Historically, interpretations of the "pierced" side of Jesus have emphasized the tragedy of innocent suffering. But understanding the internal damage wrought by hacking swords as part of God's eternal existence necessitates a deromanticization of interpretations of Christ's impaired body and a recognition of the population of people who identify with Christ's experience of disabilities, hidden and displayed, as part of our hidden history. For many people whose hidden disabilities keep them from participating fully in the church or from feeling full-bodied acceptance by Christ, accepting the disabled God may enable reconciliation with their own bodies and Christ's body the church. Hence, disability not only does not contradict the human-divine integrity, it becomes a new model of wholeness and a symbol of solidarity.

Feminist criticisms of the symbolism of Jesus as the male Galilean and lordly Christ—a problematic image for women—notwithstanding, the image of Jesus Christ, the disabled God, is not inherently oppressive for women, particularly women with disabilities. The disabled God provides a new way of identifying with the physical reality of Jesus. Clearly feminists and marginalized people cannot continue to support an

> image of Christ [which] is manipulated in the praxis of privilege (by those on the top, representatives of white male gentry) not only to symbolize the suffering servant, with whom those on the bottom can identify in terms of passive acceptance of suffering; but also, because Christ is God, to symbolize the rulership of all that is established, the guardian and custodian of all human and "natural" resources.[19]

Nonetheless, one need not move from a rejection of this image of Christ to a negation of either the physical presence or the divinity of Jesus Christ. Jesus Christ, the disabled God, is not a suffering servant or a conquering lord. Rather this contextualization of Jesus enables that "the Christ understood as the stranger, the outcast, the hungry, the weak, the poor, [and I would add person with disabilities] makes the traditional male Christ (Black and White) less significant."[20] The significance of the disabled God is not primarily maleness, but rather physicality. Jesus Christ the disabled God, is consonant with the image of Jesus Christ the stigmatized Jew, person of color, and representative of the poor and hungry— those who have struggled to maintain the integrity and dignity of their bodies in the face of the physical mutilation of injustice and rituals of bodily degradation.

Jesus Christ the disabled God, is not a romanticized notion of "overcomer" God. Instead here is God as survivor. Here language fails because the term "survivor" in our society is contaminated with notions of victimization, radical individualism, and alienation, as well as with an ethos of virtuous suffering. In contradistinction to that cultural icon, the image of survivor here evoked is that of a simple, unself-pitying, honest body, for whom the limits of power are palpable but not tragic. The disabled God embodies the ability to see clearly the complexity and the "mixed blessing" of life and bodies, without living in despair. This revelation is of a God for us who celebrates joy and experiences pain not separately in time or space, but simultaneously.

The disabled God is God for whom interdependence is not a possibility to be willed from a position of power, but a necessary condition for life. This interdependence is the fact of both justice and survival. The disabled God embodies practical interdependence, not simply willing to be interrelated from a position of power, but depending on it from a position of need. For many people with disabilities, too, mutual care is a matter of survival. To posit a Jesus Christ who needs care and mutuality as essential to human-divine survival does not symbolize either humanity or divinity as powerless. Instead it debunks the myth of individualism and hierarchical orders, in which transcendence means breaking free of encumbrances and needing nobody and constitutes the divine as somebody in relation to other bodies.

This disabled God makes possible a renewal of hope for people with disabilities and others who care. This symbol points not to a utopian vision of hope as the erasure of all human contingency, historically or eternally, for that would be to erase our bodies, our lives. Rather it is a liberatory realism that maintains a clear recognition of the limits of our bodies and an acceptance of limits as the truth of being human. This liberatory realism also calls for a realization of the necessity of a social and interpersonal transformation that does not surrender to cynicism and defeatism any more than the limits of our bodies suggest that we should do nothing. It locates our hope in justice as access and mutuality, a justice that removes the barriers which constrain our bodies, keep us excluded, and intend to humiliate us. It also situates our hope in the reality of our existence as ones with dignity and integrity. Hope is the recollection and projection that even our nonconventional bodies, which oftentimes dissatisfy and fail us, are worth the living. It is knowing that the so-called curses sometimes feel like blessings.

The image of the disabled God proceeds from Jesus Christ's embodied commitment to justice as rightly ordered interpersonal and structural relations. This is the God who indicts not only deliberate injustice, but unintended rituals of degradation that deny the full personhood of marginalized people. Moreover, Jesus

103

Christ, the disabled God, disorders the social-symbolic orders of what it means to be incarnate—in flesh—and confirms that "normal" bodies, like impaired bodies, are subject to contingency. And it is a contingency born not of tragedy or sin but of ordinary women and embodied unexceptionably. This representation of God does not gloss over the suffering enacted against bodies as the consequence of injustice; rather it posits that our bodies cannot be subsumed into injustice or sin.

The disabled God defines the church as a communion of justice. Jesus Christ, the disabled God, is as Jürgen Moltmann writes:

> The one who is to come is then already present in an anticipatory sense in history in the Spirit and the word, and in the miserable and the helpless. His future ends the world's history of suffering and completes the fragments and anticipations of his kingdom which are called the church.[21]

Thus the church, which depends for its existence on the disabled God, must live out liberating action in the world. The church finds its identity as the body of Christ only by being a community of faith and witness, a coalition of struggle and justice, and a fellowship of hope. This mission necessitates that people with disabilities be incorporated into all levels of participation and decision making.

Jesus Christ as the disabled God provides a symbolic prototype and opens the door to the theological task of re-thinking Christian symbols, metaphors, rituals, and doctrines so as to make them accessible to people with disabilities and remove their able-bodied bias. In chapter 6, the Eucharist is explored as a ritual of ordinary inclusion of people with disabilities. Liberating our theology from biases against people with disabilities is a process that will require tremendous and continual commitment to identifying with the disabled God in our midst. Even in the process of developing the symbol of Jesus Christ, disabled deity, I have heard numerous objections. Individuals who are heavily invested in a belief in the transcendence of God constituted as radical otherness will undoubtedly find this representation disconcerting. The theological implications of the disabled God resist the notion of power as absolute control over human-divine affairs. For people with disabilities who have grasped divine healing as the only liberatory image the traditional church has offered, relinquishing belief in an all-powerful God who could heal, if He would, is painful. Yet who is this god whose attention we cannot get, whose inability to respond to our pain causes still more pain? This god is surely not Emmanuel—God for us. The second objection some have expressed is that the articulation of a model of God that incorporates disability signals runaway confusion in the church, and they insist that a halt should be called on all representational language for God. With the emergence of African American, feminist, gay-lesbian, and Latin American liberation theologies in recent history, models of God have proliferated. Yet this representational proliferation does not portend chaos; rather it is the corporate enactment of the resurrection of God. The body of God is becoming alive, vivified by an insurrection of subjugated knowledges. This resurrection happens, however, only when these emerging models of God are more than simply new names for the same symbolic order. The challenge for the Christian is to engage one or more "names" of God and to follow these images into the worlds they open.

BEARING OUR BODIES

For me and, I hope, other people with disabilities, as well as for some able-bodied people, the presence of the disabled God makes it possible to bear a nonconventional body. This God enables both a struggle for justice among people with disabilities and an end to estrangement from our own bodies.

CHAPTER SIX

SACRAMENTAL BODIES

For I received from the Lord what I also handed on to you, that the Lord Jesus on the night when he was betrayed took a loaf of bread, and when he had given thanks, he broke it and said, "This is my body that is for you. Do this in remembrance of me." In the same way he took the cup also, after supper, saying, "This cup is the new covenant in my blood. Do this, as often as you drink it, in remembrance of me."

1 Corinthians 11:23-25

Do this in remembrance of me." Who is the one we remember in the Eucharist? It is the disabled God who is present at the Eucharist table—the God who was physically tortured, arose from the dead, and is present in heaven and on earth, disabled and whole. This is the dangerous memory of the crucified and resurrected one. For in Jesus' resurrection, the full and accessible presence of the disabled God is among us in our continuing human history, as people with disabilities, as the temporarily able-bodied, as church, and as communion of struggle.

Resurrection is not about the negation or erasure of our disabled bodies in hopes of perfect images, untouched by physical disability; rather Christ's resurrection offers hope that our nonconventional, and sometimes difficult, bodies participate fully in the imago Dei and that God whose nature is love and who is on the side of justice and solidarity is touched by our experience. God is changed by the experience of being a disabled body. This is what the Christian hope of resurrection means.

In the resurrection, Jesus Christ's body is not only the transfigured form that yet embodies the reality of impaired hands, feet,

107

and side; it also consists of the body whose life and unity come from the Holy Spirit active in our continuing history. In summoning us to remembrance of his body and blood at table, the disabled God calls us to liberating relationships with God, our bodies, and others. We are called to be people who work for justice and access for all and who incorporate the body practices of justice and access as part of our ordinary lives. The emancipatory transformation made possible through the person and works of the disabled God emerges from the solidarity Jesus lived out in his ministry, and it continues to be embodied as the risen Christ active in and through the church and in all who struggle for a new humanity and a more humane world. This emancipatory transformation is a liberation from sin and a calling to full participation in the life of Christ, a liberation from passivity and a calling to our own bodies, and a liberation from mutilating poverty and marginalization and a calling to be church.

THE CHURCH AS COMMUNION OF STRUGGLE

The resurrected body of Christ as the embodied church is reflected in 1 Corinthians 12:12-13, 27:

> For just as the body is one and has many members, and all the members of the body, though many, are one body, so it is with Christ. For in the one Spirit we were all baptized into one body—Jews or Greeks, slaves or free—and we were all made to drink of one Spirit. . . . Now you are the body of Christ and individually members of it.

Christ's body, the church, is broken, marked by sin, divided by disputes, and exceptional in its exclusivity. Church structures keep people with disabilities out; church officials affirm our spiritual callings but tell us there is no place for our bodies to minister; and denominations lobby to gain exception from the governmental enforcement of basic standards of justice. There is no perfect church as there is no "perfect" body.

Yet the church whose calling is to be a communion of struggle is made possible, though not made easy, by brokenness. The members of the church represent an essential diversity, interrelated by necessity and often hating the very differences that make us indispensable to one another. We recognize our differences and hold in trust our common calling as people of God, the foundation of church.

As a communion of struggle, the church's first challenge is a willingness to risk conversion. The process of repentance is vital and generally painful. Letty Russell says,

Seeing the value of diversity, both as a God-given gift of creation and also as an enrichment of our lives, becomes a possibility as we become aware of the way in which difference carries with it the negative value of dominance, of divide and conquer in our society, and take steps to change this.[1]

Naming carnal sins against people with disabilities and other bodies relegated to the margins in the church and society and taking responsibility for the body practices of the church that segregate and isolate these individuals and groups is the difficult work of making real the possibility of conversion to the disabled God. Often these processes engender conflict and tension as marginalized people seek their place in the decision-making processes of the church and make their nonconventional bodies models for ritual practice and as people who have endowed and overseen the body of the church fight to maintain control.

The church as a communion of struggle, like our bodies, is not always agreeably habitable. Just as our relations with our own bodies involve elements of struggle that cannot be eliminated, a supply of grief seldom fully dried up, and pain whose source is not always entirely evident, so, too, our relations with the church. But the church is a communion of conversion that exists as its members struggle to discern the presence of the disabled God in its midst. Only through conversion is discernment of the body of disabled God possible.

For able-bodied people, discerning the presence of God with and for people with disabilities is a struggle, indeed. Sue Halpern observes:

Physical health is contingent and often short-lived. But this truth eludes us as long as we are able to walk by simply putting one foot in front of the other. As a consequence, empathy for the disabled is unavailable to most able-bodied persons. Sympathy, yes, empathy, no, for every attempt to project oneself into that condition, to feel what it is like not to be ambulatory, for instance, is mediated by the ability to walk.[2]

Nonetheless, the experience of disability is an ever-present possibility for all people. A greater than 50 percent chance exists that an individual who is currently able-bodied will be physically disabled, either temporarily or permanently. Thus for the temporarily able-bodied, developing an empathy for people with disabilities means identifying with their own real bodies, bodies of contingency and limits.

For the most part, the bodies of the temporarily able-bodied do not conform to the idealized bodies upheld by sports-shoe commercials and magazine covers. Real bodies are seldom the icons of health and physical attractiveness that popular culture parades as "normal." Yet these are the bodies of desire and imagination. As Susan Wendell writes:

Idealizing the body prevents everyone, able-bodied and disabled, from identifying with and loving her/his real body. Some people can have the illusion of acceptance that comes from believing that their bodies are "close enough" to the ideal, but this illusion only draws them deeper into identifying with the ideal and into the endless task of reconciling the reality with it. Sooner or later they must fail.[3]

In struggling to identify with the disabled God, temporarily able-bodied people work to become known to themselves as their actually existing bodies. Breaking the silence about their real lives as bodies makes possible a "return to the body"—a positive body awareness that comes not from pursuing an ideal but from accepting the reality that bodies evolve, become ill and disabled, and die.[4] As the church becomes the site for the difficult work of finding that oneself includes a body, the temporarily able-bodied as well as people with disabilities may come to understand what bodily integrity means as a spiritual and physical practice. Conversion then is, in part, learning to love what is carnal and our own already existing body.

Awareness of our bodies has taught people with disabilities about the reality of injustice in the world and in the church. Thus we seek in the church a communion of struggle for justice. It is the church "already" in its recognition that struggle is necessary and its willingness to engage the struggle. It is the church "not yet" in the realization that the rigors of discernment and the work to change structures and attitudes that cause marginalization, exclusion, and exploitation and to heal wounds those structures and attitudes inflict will not be finished so far as can now be seen. The struggle for justice entails the physical practices of relating to and caring for people with disabilities as central to the mission of the church. It entails making program, buildings, and ritual spaces accessible for those whose bodies need specific care. It means creating and supporting paid positions for advocacy within denominational structures. Justice for people with disabilities requires that the theological and ritual foundations of the church be shaken. As it communes together, the church emboldens and enlivens the struggle for justice within existing church institutions and the struggle for a transformation of church and social structures.

EUCHARIST AS BODY PRACTICE

This struggle for justice is part of the ordinary life of the church.[5] The struggle for wholeness and justice begins with the practices and habits of the church itself. As noted in chapter 3, the Christian church has not only been complacent to the struggle of people with disabilities, it has too long provided the ideological funding and charitable practices that have marginalized us in society. The church is thus called first to discern the presence of the disabled God in its midst.

One place to begin is to consider the body practices of the church. The body practices of the church are a physical language—the routines, rules, and practices of the body, conscious and unconscious. In the church, the body practices are the physical discourse of inclusion and exclusion. These practices reveal the hidden "membership roll," those whose bodies matter in the shaping of liturgies and services.

Receiving the Eucharist is a body practice of the church. The Eucharist as a central and constitutive practice of the church is a ritual of membership. Someone who can take or serve communion is a real Christian subject. Hence inclusion of people with disabilities in the ordinary practice of receiving and administering the Eucharist is a matter of bodily mediation of justice and an incorporation of hope.

My reflections on the practice of giving and receiving the Eucharist come from my own experience in several congregations and from the experience of other people with disabilities. The bodily practice of receiving the Eucharist in most congregations includes filing to the front of the sanctuary and kneeling at the communion rail. When I initially attended services, I would often be alerted by an usher that I need not go forward for the Eucharist. Instead I would be offered the sacrament at my seat when everyone else had been served. My presence in the service using either a wheelchair or crutches made problematical the "normal" bodily practice of the Eucharist in the congregation. Yet rather than focusing on the congregation's practices that excluded my body and asking, "How do we alter the bodily practice of the Eucharist in order that this individual and others with disabilities would have full access to the ordinary practices of the church?" the decision makers would center the (unstated) problem on my disabled body, asking, "How should we accommodate this person with a disability in our practice of Eucharist?" Hence receiving the Eucharist was transformed for me from a corporate to a solitary experience; from a sacralization of Christ's broken body to a stigmatization of my disabled body.

The exclusion and segregation of people with disabilities from receiving and administering the Eucharist has been the "normal" practice of the church. The experience of other people with disabilities bears witness to this hidden history. Stuart Govig, a theologian with disabilities, writes of being denied entrance to seminary until he could prove that he could perform the eucharistic ritual appropriately, meaning without altering the able-bodied practice.[6] Marilynn Phillips recounts the religious experience of Margaret Orlinski, a young Polish-American woman with polio. Margaret reports her ambiguous relations within the Christian community. "I was called a saint. 'God loves her so much to have given her this cross to bear.' I heard that so many times. I felt an enormous amount of pressure to be perfect because I was 'one of God's favorites.'"[7] On the other hand, Margaret's impairment made her different and led to her segregation.

> For First Holy Communion, ordinarily an event celebrating one's spiritual growth in the collective setting of one's age peers, Margaret not only was tutored separately but also received the sacrament not in the church, but in an individualized ceremony in her home. Although the event was not celebrated in the traditional manner, among age peers and in the church, nevertheless it was designated for collective celebration: "People flooded the living room with tears! Here's this little crippled, pathetic girl receiving Jesus for the first time!"[8]

For many people with disabilities, the Eucharist is a ritual of exclusion and degradation. Access to this celebration of the body is restricted because of architectural barriers, ritual practices, demeaning body aesthetics, unreflective speech, and bodily reactions. Hence the Eucharist becomes a dreaded and humiliating remembrance that in the church we are trespassers in an able-bodied dominion. For many people at the margins of the institutional church, the Eucharist is what Letty M. Russell identifies as "a sacrament of disunion."[9] In making the Eucharist a physical practice of exclusion, the church demonstrates a tangible bias against our nonconventional bodies and dishonors the disabled God.

113

Instead, the Eucharist must become a bodily practice of justice. Russell says:

> The sacraments are about God reaching out on the cross, to make things right, and about God's continuing action on behalf of groaning creation. Here we find the gift of righteousness and justice and are called to right administration of those gifts, together with others in need of God's justice within and beyond the rubrics of our particular traditions.[10]

Hope and the possibility of liberation welling up from a broken body is the miracle of the Eucharist. At the table, we remember the physical reality of that body broken for a people broken. At the table, we understand that Christ is present with us. As the disabled God, Christ has brought us grace and, in turn, makes us a grace to others as physical beings.

Jesus Christ, the disabled God and the incarnation of hope, requires that eucharistic theology and ritual be a sacrament of actually existing bodies. It is the beginning of discerning and remembering the disabled God in the body practices of the church and situating our struggle for justice within the church. As a sacrament of the church, the Eucharist is an outward and visible sign of a physical and spiritual grace. It is prophetic symbol, realizing and celebrating the presence and action of God. It is a bodily practice of grace.

Hence a body practice of Eucharist that excludes or segregates people with disabilities is not a celebration of the real body of Christ. Gutiérrez suggests,

> Without a real commitment against exploitation and alienation and for a society of solidarity and justice, the Eucharistic celebration is an empty action, lacking any genuine endorsement by those who participate in it.[11]

The eucharistic practices of the church must make real our remembrance of the disabled God by making good on body practices of access and inclusion. For some eucharistic traditions, this commitment will necessitate changes in the "normal" rituals of institution that exclude ministers with disabilities from presiding at Holy Communion. For others, it will enjoin kneeling as the "normal" posture of the ritual. For all traditions, it means constituting eucharistic rituals so as to discontinue the exclusionary body practices that treat people with disabilities as exceptions to the rule or deviants. Through the Eucharist, people with disabilities reject the church's stigmatization of our nonconventional bodies and call for its reconciliation with the disabled God.

Incarnating the disabled God through the Eucharist also means affirming the unexpected participant. Emerging from the Seder, the Eucharist involves welcoming the invisible guest, that is, opening the door to Elijah. For people with disabilities who have been visible but invisible, seen and stigmatized but not acknowledged, Eucharist as a body practice of justice and inclusion welcomes us and recognizes the church's impairment when we are not included. The church is impoverished without our presence. Our narratives and bodies make clear that ordinary lives incorporate contingency and difficulty. We reveal the physical truth of embodiment as a painstaking process of claiming and inhabiting our actually existing bodies. People with disabilities in the church announce the presence of the disabled God for us and call the church to become a communion of struggle.

An altered body practice of the Eucharist is the evidence that the grace of God comes through bodies. Hence, it is at once a call for justice and a recognition of the value of nonconventional bodies. Often the Eucharist institutes a glorification of suffering, rather than a repudiation of injustice and an affirmation of the potency of the body. A call for justice comes from the disabled God's experience of torture. Acts of injustice are also inscribed on the bodies of many people with disabilities. War and malnutrition as major causes of disability underscore the role of injustice in creating disabled bodies. Nonetheless, the Eucharist symbolizes that our nonconventional bodies cannot be reduced to artifacts of injustice and sin. Most people with disabilities see our bodies not as signs of deviance or deformity, but as images of beauty and wholeness. We discern in our bodies, not only the ravages of injustice and pain, but also the reality of surviving with dignity. We,

115

who through the Eucharist meditate on Jesus Christ, the disabled God, recognize in ourselves the imago Dei. We see in Christ the affirmation of nonconventional bodies.

The Eucharist as body practice signifies solidarity and reconciliation: God among humankind, the temporarily able-bodied with people with disabilities, and we ourselves with our own bodies. In the Eucharist, we encounter the disabled God, who displayed the signs of disability, not as a demonstration of failure and defect, but in affirmation of connection and strength. In this resurrected Christ, the nonconventional body is recognized as sacrament. Christ's solidarity with the more than 600 million people with disabilities worldwide is revealed in the Eucharist.

This understanding of the Eucharist, therefore, must reject the image of the "perfect body" as an oppressive myth. In the United States where a fetish for perfect bodies drives people to self-flagellation in overzealous exercise, to mutilation through plastic surgery, to disablement in eating disorders, and to warehousing and stigmatizing people with disabilities, young and old, the eucharistic message that affirms actually existing bodies is desperately needed and offers healing body practices. This affirmation differs from a romanticization of the body, male or female. Instead it acknowledges the ambiguous character of embodiment and affirms our existence as painstakingly, honestly, and lovingly embodied beings.

LAYING ON OF HANDS

Reconceiving the body practices of the church necessitates that other physical rituals be examined, as well. As a person reared in a Pentecostal church, I have great appreciation for body practices such as laying on of hands, practices largely absent from the worship services of many denominations. Yet the practice of laying on of hands can become an ordinary ritual of inclusion for people with disabilities. Our bodies have too often been touched by hands that have forgotten our humanity and attend only to curing us. A religious body ritual that redeems our bodies from mechanistic practices of rehabilitative medicine enables us to connect with our bodies as spiritual forms. Such experiences have transformative power.

My own history with laying on of hands has been an ambiguous one. Often the practice has been closely associated with ritual healing. I, like many people with disabilities, have experienced the negative effects of healing rituals. Healing has been the churchly parallel to rehabilitative medicine, in which the goal was "normalization" of the bodies of people with disabilities. As Nancy J. Lane writes, "Healing is expected to change the person who has a disability into one who does not. The burden of healing is placed totally on the person who is disabled, causing further suffering and continued alienation from the Church."[12] Failure to be "healed" is often assessed as a personal flaw in the individual, such as unrepentant sin or a selfish desire to remain disabled. Thus for many people with disabilities, laying on of hands is associated with their stigmatization within the church.

Yet I have also experienced laying on of hands that was restorative and redemptive. These physical mediations of God's grace have often kept me related to my body at times when all of my impulses pushed me toward dissociating from the pain-wracked, uncomfortable beast. For example, as a child after spending several months in hospitals having my body rebuilt surgically, I was a participant in a powerful service of laying on of hands. In a charismatic meeting in a rural North Dakota parish, I experienced the body care of several elderly nuns schooled in physical attendance as nurses and touched by the spirit as Christians. Their touch and tears were the body practices of inclusion. My body belonged in the church. From that early age, I recall the physical sensation of having my body redeemed for God as those spiritual women laid hands on me, caressing my pain, lifting my isolation, and revealing my spiritual body. For people with disabilities, such experiences of physical redemption and ordinary inclusion are rare.

The work to create rituals of bodily inclusion is vital to the church as a communion of struggle. The efforts to recover the hidden history of people with disabilities and to restore our bodies within the church is our conversion to the disabled God. The

117

eucharistic prayer offered here is part of my own struggle to practice my body as sacred space with other believers. This ritual is generally accompanied by reciprocal laying on of hands as the Eucharist is administered and received. It is offered here as illustration of new bodily practices that create liberating spaces and rituals for our sacramental bodies.

A EUCHARISTIC PRACTICE

Let us place ourselves in the presence of the disabled God and ask ourselves—how is God with us?

[God,] it was you who formed my inward parts;
    you knit me together in my mother's womb.
I praise you, for I am fearfully and wonderfully made.
    Wonderful are your works;
that I know very well.
    My frame was not hidden from you,
When I was being made in secret,
    intricately woven in the depths of the earth.
Your eyes beheld my unformed substance.
In your book were written
    all the days that were formed for me
    when none of them as yet existed.

(From Psalm 139)

May God be with you.
And also with you.
Open yourselves to God and one another.
We open ourselves to God and one another.
The time is right to remember our God. ·
Thanks be to God.
Wise and gracious God, Creator of all good things, Redeemer of this broken world, you who are present with your people and the earth itself, we pray to you.
Remembering . . . the truth about your fear and anger and grief. You were forsaken and ignored and depressed.

118

We pray to you, the source of love in the world, the beginning of justice in history, the origin of peace on earth. You are God for us. *Remembering . . . the binds and bonds of your body. You create the space of encounter, the holiness of supping from another's cup, and the ambivalence of breaking.*

You lead your people out of bondage into freedom. You receive us into your body and we are made complete. You make the wounds part of the whole body. We pray to you.

Remembering . . . we have nothing but our flesh to offer you for yours. You give us ourselves and you risk everything.

All: We remember that on the night before Jesus was executed by those who feared both him and you, he ate a Passover meal with his friends, in celebration of liberation of your people from bondage. Remembering your power, Jesus took bread, and blessed it, and broke it, and gave it to his friends and said, "Take. Eat. This is my body, which will be broken for you. Whenever you eat it, remember me."

After supper, he took the wine, blessed it, and gave it to them, and said, "Drink this. This is my blood which will be shed for you, and for others, for the forgiveness of sins, to heal and empower you. Whenever you drink it, remember me."

Remembering Jesus in the breaking of his body and spilling of his blood, we ask you to bless this bread and this wine, making it for us the Body and Blood of Jesus the Christ, the disabled God. Bless us also that we may be for you living members of Christ's body in the world.[13]

NOTES

ACKNOWLEDGMENTS

1. Nancy Mairs, *Carnal Acts: Essays* (New York: HarperCollins, 1990), p. 130.

CHAPTER ONE: COMING TO TERMS

1. Rebecca S. Chopp, "Practical Theology and Liberation," in L. S. Mudge and J. N. Poling (eds.), *Formation and Reflection* (Philadelphia: Fortress Press, 1987), pp. 130-31.
2. Rebecca S. Chopp, *The Power to Speak* (New York: Crossroads, 1989), p. 7.
3. David Tracy, "Practical Theology in the Situation of Global Pluralism," in L. S. Mudge and J. N. Poling (eds.), *Formation and Reflection* (Philadelphia: Fortress Press, 1987), pp. 139-40.
4. Chopp, "Practical Theology and Liberation," p. 132.
5. Bryan S. Turner, *The Body and Society: Explorations in Social Theory* (Oxford: Basil Blackwell, 1984), p. 41.
6. Paul Ricoeur, *The Symbolism of Evil.* Emerson Buchanan, trans. (Boston: Beacon Press, 1967), p. 348.
7. Ibid.
8. The designation "temporarily able-bodied" (TAB) has become a common term for able-bodied persons or "normals" within the disability community.
9. J. Gliedman and W. Roth, *The Unexpected Minority: Handicapped Children in America* (New York: Harcourt Brace Jovanovich, 1980), p. 5.
10. See Constantina Safilios-Rothschild, "Disabled Persons Self-Definition and Their Implications for Rehabilitation," in G. Albrecht (ed.), *The Sociology of Physical Disability and Rehabilitation* (Pittsburgh: University of Pittsburgh Press, 1976), pp. 9-56; Harlan Hahn, "Civil Rights for Disabled Americans: The Foundation of a Political Agenda," in A. Gartner and T. Joe (eds.), *Images of the Disabled, Disabling Images* (New York: Praeger, 1987), pp. 181-203.
11. Safilios-Rothschild, "Disabled Persons Self-Definition," p. 39.
12. Nancy Mairs, *Plaintext* (Tucson: University of Arizona, 1986), p. 11.
13. Ibid., p. 10.

14. Paul K. Longmore, "A Note on the Language and the Social Identity of Disabled People," *American Behavioral Scientist* 28 (1985): 420.
15. J. Scheer and N. Groce, "Impairment as a Human Constant: Cross-Cultural and Historical Perspectives on Variation," *Journal of Social Issues* 44 (1988): 24.
16. S. Z. Nagi, "The Concept and Measurement of Disability in Disability Policies and Government Programs," in E. D. Berkowitz (ed.), *Disability Policies and Government Programs* (New York: Praeger, 1979), p. 3.
17. Hahn, "Civil Rights for Disabled Americans," p. 189.
18. See Longmore, "A Note on the Language"; Frank Bowe, *Handicapping America: Barriers to Disabled People* (New York: Harper & Row, Publishers, 1978).

CHAPTER TWO: BODIES OF KNOWLEDGE

1. Alfred Schutz, "On Multiple Realities," *Collected Papers*, vol. 1 (The Hague: Martinus Nijhoff, 1962), pp. 222-23.
2. Adrienne Rich, *Of Woman Born: Motherhood as Experience and Institution* (New York: Norton, 1976), p. 39. Rich addresses this as the "corporeal ground of intelligence."
3. Geyla Frank, *Venus on Wheels: The Life History of a Congenital Amputee* (Ph.D. Dissertation, Department of Anthropology, University of California, Los Angeles, 1981).
4. Nancy Mairs, *Plaintext* (Tucson: University of Arizona, 1986); *Remembering the Bone House: An Erotics of Place and Space* (New York: Harper & Row, Publishers, 1989); *Carnal Acts* (New York: HarperCollins, 1990); and *Ordinary Time: Cycles in Marriage, Faith and Renewal* (Boston: Beacon Press, 1993).
5. Geyla Frank, "On Embodiment: A Case Study of Congenital Limb Deficiency in American Culture," in Michelle Fine and Adrienne Asch (eds.), *Women with Disabilities: Essays in Psychology, Culture and Politics* (Philadelphia: Temple University Press, 1988), pp. 45-46.
6. Geyla Frank, "Beyond Stigma: Visibility and Self-Empowerment of Persons with Congenital Limb Deficiencies," *Journal of Social Issues* 44 (1988): 98.
7. Ibid., 99.
8. Frank, "On Embodiment," pp. 47-48.
9. Geyla Frank, "'Becoming the Other': Empathy and Biographical Interpretation," *Biography* 8 (1985): 200.
10. Frank, "Beyond Stigma," 107.
11. Ibid.
12. Frank, "On Embodiment," p. 54.
13. Ibid., p. 51.
14. Ibid.
15. Frank, *Venus on Wheels*, p. 186.
16. Frank, "On Embodiment," p. 65.
17. Frank, *Venus on Wheels*.
18. Mairs, *Carnal Acts*, p. 18.

19. Mairs, *Remembering the Bone House,* p. 241.
20. Ibid., p. 240.
21. Ibid., p. 241.
22. Ibid., p. 250.
23. Ibid., p. 252.
24. Mairs, *Plaintext,* pp. 11-12.
25. Ibid., p. 12.
26. Mairs, *Remembering the Bone House,* pp. 234-35.
27. Mairs, *Carnal Acts,* pp. 88-89.
28. Mairs, *Ordinary Time,* p. 25.
29. Mairs, *Carnal Acts,* p. 17.
30. Ibid., p. 96.
31. Mairs, *Ordinary Time,* pp. 17-32.
32. Ibid., pp. 167-68.
33. Ibid.
34. Mairs, *Carnal Acts,* p. 111.
35. Ibid., p. 114.
36. Mairs, *Ordinary Time,* pp. 216-17.
37. Mairs, *Plaintext,* p. 20.

CHAPTER THREE: THE BODY POLITICS

1. Michel Foucault, *Power/Knowledge: Selected Interviews and Other Writings 1972–1977* (New York: Pantheon, 1980), p. 172.
2. Richard K. Scotch, *From Good Will to Civil Rights* (Philadelphia: Temple University Press, 1984), p. 20.
3. Richard K. Scotch, "Disability as the Basis for a Social Movement: Advocacy and the Politics of Definition," *Journal of Social Issues* 44 (1988): 163.
4. Thalidomide was the anti–morning sickness drug used by pregnant women. Diane Driedger, *The Last Civil Rights Movement: Disabled Peoples' International* (New York: St. Martin's Press, 1989), p. 8.
5. For an in-depth discussion of rehabilitation in federal legislation, see Edward D. Berkowitz, *Disabled Policy: America's Programs for the Handicapped* (New York: Cambridge University Press, 1987); Stephen Percy, *Disability, Civil Rights and Public Policy: The Politics of Implementation* (Tuscaloosa: University of Alabama Press, 1989); and Gary L. Albrecht (ed.), *Cross National Rehabilitation Policies: A Sociological Perspective* (Beverly Hills: SAGE Press, 1981).
6. Gary Albrecht, "Socialization and the Disability Process" in Gary Albrecht (ed.), *The Sociology of Physical Disability and Rehabilitation* (Pittsburgh: University of Pittsburgh Press, 1976), p. 269.
7. Berkowitz, *Disabled Policy,* p. 155.
8. Gary L. Albrecht and Judith A. Levy, "Constructing Disabilities as Social Problems" in Albrecht (ed.), *Cross National Rehabilitation Policies,* p. 22.

9. Robert Funk, "Disability Rights: From Caste to Class in the Context of Civil Rights" in Alan Gartner and Tom Joe (eds.), *Images of the Disabled, Disabling Images* (New York: Praeger, 1987), p. 13.

10. For more extensive analysis of the genesis of the disability rights movement, see Richard K. Scotch, "Politics and Policy in the History of the Disability Rights Movement," *Milbank Quarterly,* 1989, vol. 67, suppl. 2 (no. 2): 380-400; Joseph P. Shapiro, *No Pity: People with Disabilities Forging a New Civil Rights Movement* (New York: Times Books, 1993).

11. Quoted in Driedger, *The Last Civil Rights Movement,* pp. 21-22. The independent living movement, which initially addressed primarily the quality of life concerns of its middle-class, educated founders, also included in its political agenda issues of poverty and social discrimination vital to people with disabilities in general.

12. Scotch, "Disability as the Basis for a Social Movement," 164.

13. Scotch, *From Good Will to Civil Rights,* p. 36.

14. Scotch, "Disability as the Basis for a Social Movement," 166.

15. Scotch, *From Good Will to Civil Rights,* p. 9.

16. Americans with Disabilities Act, 101st Cong. (1990), 2nd sess., 3. *U.S. Statutes at Large,* vol. 104, 329.

17. Lee Meyerson, "The Social Psychology of Physical Disability: 1948 and 1988," *Journal of Social Issues* 44 (1988): 173.

18. Michael Oliver, *The Politics of Disablement: A Sociological Approach* (New York: St. Martin's Press, 1990), p. 64.

19. R. Silver and C. Wortman, "Coping with Undesirable Life Events" in J. Gerber and M. Seligman (eds.), *Human Helplessness, Theory and Applications* (London: Academic Press, 1980).

20. Irving Zola, "Social and Cultural Disincentives to Independent Living," *Archives of Physical Medicine and Rehabilitation,* vol. 63 (1982), 84.

21. Erving Goffman, *Stigma: Notes on the Management of Spoiled Identity* (New York: Simon and Schuster, 1963).

22. Ibid., p. 5.

23. Ibid., pp. 10-11.

24. Ibid., p. 7.

25. Victor Finkelstein, *Attitudes and Disabled People: Issues for Discussion* (New York: World Rehabilitation Fund, 1980).

26. Barney G. Glaser and Anselm L. Strauss, *The Discovery of Grounded Theory: Strategies for Qualitative Research* (Chicago: Aldine, 1967), pp. 136-39.

27. Z. Gussow and G. Tracy, "The Role of Self-Help Clubs in Adaptation to Chronic Illness and Disability," *Social Science and Medicine* 10 (1968): 316.

28. Joan Ablon, "Stigmatized Health Conditions," *Social Science and Medicine,* 15B (1981): 8.

29. Roger Barker, "The Social Psychology of Physical Disability," *Journal of Social Issues* 4 (1948): 36.

30. For alternative constructions of the minority model of disability, see John Gliedman and William Roth, *The Unexpected Minority: Handicapped Children in America* (New York: Harcourt Brace Jovanovich, 1980); Harlan Hahn, "Civil Rights for Disabled Americans: The Foundation of a Political Agenda" in Alan Gartner and Tom Joe (eds.), *Images of the Disabled, Disabling Images* (New York: Praeger, 1987), and "Politics of Physical Difference," *Journal of Social Issues* 44 (1988): 39-47; and Scotch, *From Good Will to Civil Rights* and "Disability as the Basis for a Social Movement."

31. L. Wirth, "The Problem of Minority Groups" in M. Kurokawa (ed.), *Minority Responses: Comparative Views of Reactions to Subordination* (New York: Random House, 1970), p. 34.

32. Ellen C. Wertlieb, "Minority Group Status of the Disabled," *Human Relations* 38 (11): 1048.

33. Constantina Safilios-Rothschild, *The Sociology and Social Psychology of Disability and Rehabilitation* (New York: Random House, 1970), p. 110.

34. Ibid., p. 111.

35. National Center for Health Statistics, *Health, United States, 1989* (Hyattsville, Md.: U.S. Public Health Service, 1990), DHHS Pub. No (PHS) 90-1232.

36. National Institute on Disability Rehabilitation Research, *Chartbook on Disability in the United States,* An InfoUse Report (Washington, D.C.: U.S. Government Printing Office, 1989).

37. From research by W. J. Hanna and B. Rogovsky, reported in Adrienne Asch and Michelle Fine, "Introduction: Beyond Pedestals" in Michelle Fine and Adrienne Asch (eds.), *Women with Disabilities: Essays in Psychology, Culture and Politics* (Philadelphia: Temple University Press, 1988), pp. 13-14.

38. Ibid.

39. Stephen Holmes, *New York Times,* September 30, 1991, A8.

CHAPTER FOUR: CARNAL SINS

1. Gustavo Gutiérrez, *A Theology of Liberation.* 15th Anniversary edition (Maryknoll, N.Y.: Orbis, 1988), p. 147.

2. O. Tempkin, quoted in Bryan S. Turner, *The Body and Society* (Oxford: Basil Blackwell, 1984), p. 68.

3. The American Lutheran Church (ALC) merged with the Lutheran Church in America (LCA) in 1987, forming the Evangelical Lutheran Church in America (ELCA). I have retained this case study, despite the dissolution of the acting body, because the ALC created a "paper trail," documenting the contradictions between their requirements for ministerial candidates and their position on the full inclusion of people with disabilities. Furthermore, the adoption of the restrictive ministerial qualifications by the ALC created a political firestorm within the disability rights movement. The denomination's action was interpreted as a glaring example of how people with disabilities are seen by the church as appropriate objects of ministry, but unacceptable subjects of ministry. This incident became a rallying point for

many individuals within the disability community concerning our marginal position within religious institutions.

4. Gutiérrez, *A Theology of Liberation*, p. 116.

5. American Lutheran Church, Action General Convention 80.6.109.

6. American Lutheran Church, "Seminary Admission and Certification Requirements in Relation to the Work ALC Pastors are Expected to Do," *Lutheran Standard* (May 3 and July 12, 1985).

7. American Lutheran Church, Action General Convention 80.6.109.

8. Quoted in J. Lischer and L. Lischer, "No Handicapped Ministers Need Apply," *Christian Century* 102 (1985): 670.

9. Ibid.

10. Michael Oliver, *The Politics of Disablement: A Sociological Approach* (New York: St. Martin's Press, 1990), p. 115.

11. Diane Driedger, *The Last Civil Rights Movement: Disabled Peoples' International* (New York: St. Martin's Press, 1989), pp. 97-98.

12. Ibid., p. 98.

13. Leslie Fiedler, *Pity and Fear: Images of the Disabled in Literature and the Popular Arts* (United Nations: International Center for the Disabled, 1981), p. 1.

14. Robert Funk, "Disability Rights: From Caste to Class in the Context of Civil Rights" in Alan Gartner and Tom Joe (eds.), *Images of the Disabled, Disabling Images* (New York: Praeger, 1987), p. 18.

15. American Lutheran Church, "Disability Within the Family of God: A Theology of Access" (Minneapolis, 1980), 14.

16. See bell hooks, *Talking Back* (Boston: South End Press, 1989), p. 15.

17. Ibid.

18. Ibid.

19. American Lutheran Church, "Disability Within the Family of God: A Theology of Access," 14.

20. Gutiérrez, *A Theology of Liberation*, p. 57.

21. American Lutheran Church, "Disability Within the Family of God," 2.

22. Ibid., 3.

23. Ibid.

24. Viktor Frankl, quoted in American Lutheran Church, "Disability Within the Family of God," 8.

25. American Lutheran Church, "Disability Within the Family of God," 4.

26. Ibid., 7.

27. Ibid., 12.

CHAPTER FIVE: THE DISABLED GOD

1. Carter Heyward, *Our Passion for Justice* (New York: Pilgrim Press, 1984), p. 145.

2. Rebecca Chopp, *The Power to Speak* (New York: Crossroads, 1989), p. 117.

3. Clifford Geertz, *The Interpretation of Cultures: Selected Essays* (New York: Basic Books, 1973), p. 90.

4. Carol Christ, "Why Women Need the Goddess: Phenomenological, Psychological, and Political Reflections," in C. Christ and J. Plaskow (eds.), *Womanspirit Rising: A Feminist Reader in Religion* (San Francisco: Harper & Row, Publishers, 1979), p. 275.

5. Iris Marion Young, *Justice and the Politics of Difference* (Princeton: Princeton University Press, 1990), p. 148.

6. Erving Goffman, *Stigma: Notes on the Management of Spoiled Identity* (Englewood Cliffs: Prentice Hall, 1963).

7. Young, *Justice and the Politics of Difference*, p. 59.

8. Chopp, *The Power to Speak*, p. 7.

9. Young, *Justice and the Politics of Difference*, p. 147.

10. Nancy Mairs, *Carnal Acts* (New York: HarperCollins, 1990), p. 18.

11. Audre Lorde, *Sister Outsider* (Trumansburg, N.Y.: Crossing Press, 1984), pp. 56-57.

12. Ibid., p. 57.

13. "Malnutrition Disables 100 Million," *One World* 62:13.

14. Quoted in R. Funk, "Disability Rights: From Caste to Class in the Context of Civil Rights" in A. Gartner and T. Joe (eds.), *Images of the Disabled, Disabling Images* (New York: Praeger, 1987), p. 23.

15. In "Metaphor and Symbol," Ricoeur qualifies his earlier position. "Today I am less certain that one can attack the problem so directly without first having taken linguistics into account. Within the symbol, it now seems to me, there is something non-semantic." Paul Ricoeur, *Interpretation Theory: Discourse and the Surplus of Meaning* (Fort Worth: Texas Christian University Press, 1976), p. 45. Yet the approach employed here is consonant with Ricoeur's approach. Ricoeur understands the dynamic of reading the biblical text as a challenge for the reader to engage one or more "names" of God and to follow these epithets into "worlds" that the text then opens.

16. Orlando E. Costas, *Christ Outside the Gate: Mission Beyond Christendom* (Maryknoll, N.Y.: Orbis Books, 1989), p. 5.

17. Nancy Mairs, *Ordinary Time* (Boston: Beacon Press, 1993), p. 3.

18. Raymond Brown, *The Birth of the Messiah: A Commentary on the Infancy Narratives in Matthew and Luke* (Garden City, N.Y.: Doubleday Image Books, 1979), p. 26. Brown contends that the earliest Christian preaching about Jesus concerned his death and resurrection.

19. Heyward, *Our Passion for Justice*, p. 215.

20. Jacquelyn Grant, *White Women's Christ and Black Women's Jesus: Feminist Christology and Womanist Response* (Atlanta: Scholars Press, 1989), p. 219.

21. Jürgen Moltmann, *The Church in the Power of the Spirit: A Contribution to Messianic Ecclesiology* (San Francisco: Harper & Row, Publishers, 1977), p. 132.

CHAPTER SIX: SACRAMENTAL BODIES

1. Letty M. Russell, *Church in the Round: Feminist Interpretation of the Church* (Louisville: Westminster/John Knox Press, 1993), p. 160.

2. Sue Halpern, "Portrait of the Artist," Review of *Under the Eye of the Clock* by Christopher Nolan. *New York Review of Books,* June 30, 1988, 3-4.

3. Susan Wendell, "Toward a Feminist Theory of Disability," *Hypatia* 4 (2): 112.

4. Barbara Hillyer, *Feminism and Disability* (Norman, Okla.: University of Oklahoma Press, 1993), p. 171.

5. I am indebted to Bobbi Patterson for the following understanding of the ordinary body practices of the church.

6. Stuart Govig, "Children of a Lesser God," *Dialog* 24 (1985): 246.

7. Marilynn Phillips, "Disability and Ethnicity in Conflict: A Study of Transformation," in M. Fine and A. Asch (eds.), *Women with Disabilities* (Philadelphia: Temple University Press, 1988), p. 206.

8. Ibid., pp. 206-7.

9. Russell, *Church in the Round,* p. 142.

10. Ibid., p. 145.

11. Gustavo Gutiérrez, *A Theology of Liberation,* 15th Anniversary ed. (Maryknoll, N.Y.: Orbis Books, 1988), p. 150.

12. Nancy J. Lane, "Healing Bodies and Victimization of Persons: Issues of Faith-Healing for Persons with Disabilities," *The Disability Rag Resource* 14 (3): 12.

13. Adapted from Carter Heyward, *Our Passion for Justice: Images of Power, Sexuality, and Liberation* (New York: Pilgrim Press, 1984), pp. 149-50. Reprinted by permission of The Pilgrim Press, Cleveland, Ohio, as found in OUR PASSION FOR JUSTICE: IMAGES OF POWER, SEXUALITY, AND LIBERATION by Carter Heyward, copyright 1984.

SELECTED BIBLIOGRAPHY

Ablon, J.
1981   "Stigmatized Health Conditions." *Social Science and Medicine.* 15B:5-9.
Albrecht, G. L.
1976   "Socialization and the Disability Process." In G. L. Albrecht (ed.), *The Sociology of Physical Disability and Rehabilitation* (pp. 3-38). University of Pittsburgh Press.
1976   "Social Policy and the Management of Human Resources." In G. L. Albrecht (ed.), *The Sociology of Physical Disability and Rehabilitation* (pp. 257-85). University of Pittsburgh Press.
1981   *Cross National Rehabilitation Policies: A Sociological Perspective.* Beverly Hills: SAGE Press.
Albrecht, G. L., and J. Levy
1981   "Constructing Disabilities as Social Problems." In G. Albrecht (ed.), *Cross National Rehabilitation Policies: A Sociological Perspective.* Beverly Hills: SAGE Press.
American Lutheran Church
1980   "Disability Within the Family of God: A Theology of Access for the American Lutheran Church." Minneapolis, Minnesota.
1985   "Seminary Admission and Certification Requirements in Relation to the Work ALC Pastors Are Expected to Do." *Lutheran Standard* (May 3 and July 12, 1985).
1986   Reports and Actions, Part I, Action General Convention, 80.6.109.
Americans with Disabilities Act
1990   *U.S. Statutes at Large.* Vol. 104 (pp. 327-78).
Anspach, R. R.
1979   "From Stigma to Identity Politics: Political Activism Among the Physically Disabled and Former Mental Patients." *Social Science and Medicine* 13:765-73.

Asch A., and M. Fine
  1988   "Introduction: Beyond Pedestals." In M. Fine and A. Asch (eds.),
          Women with Disabilities: Essays in Psychology, Culture and Politics (pp.
          1-37). Philadelphia: Temple University Press.

Barker, R. G.
  1948   "The Social Psychology of Physical Disability." *Journal of Social Issues*
          4:28-38.
Barker, R. G., B. A. Wright, L. Meyerson, and M. R. Gonick
  1953   *Adjustment to Physical Handicap and Illness: A Survey of the Social
          Psychology of Physique and Disability.* New York: Social Science Research
          Council.
Berkowitz, E. D.
  1987   *Disabled Policy: America's Programs for the Handicapped.* New York:
          Cambridge University Press.
Berkowitz, M., W. G. Johnson, and E. H. Murphy
  1976   *Public Policy Toward Disability.* New York: Praeger.
Blaxter, M.
  1976   *The Meaning of Disability: A Sociological Study of Impairment.* London:
          Heinemann.
Bowe, F.
  1978   *Handicapping America: Barriers to Disabled People.* New York: Harper &
          Row, Publishers.
  1980   *Rehabilitating America: Toward Independence for Disabled and Elderly
          People.* New York: Harper & Row, Publishers.
  1981   *Comeback: Six Remarkable People Who Triumphed Over Disability.* New
          York: Harper & Row, Publishers.
Brechen, A., P. Liddiard, and J. Swain
  1981   *Handicap in a Social World.* Kent, England: Hodder and Stoughton.
Brown, R.
  1979   *The Birth of the Messiah: A Commentary on the Infancy Narratives in
          Matthew and Luke.* Garden City, N.Y.: Doubleday Image Books.

Chopp, R. S.
  1987   "Practical Theology and Liberation." In L. S. Mudge and J. N. Poling
          (eds.), *Formation and Reflection* (pp. 120-38). Philadelphia: Fortress
          Press.
  1989   *The Power to Speak.* New York: Crossroads.
Christ, C.
  1979   "Why Women Need the Goddess: Phenomenological, Psychological,
          and Political Reflections." In C. Christ and J. Plaskow (eds.),
          Womanspirit Rising: A Feminist Reader in Religion (pp. 273-87). San
          Francisco: Harper & Row, Publishers.
Colston, L. G.
  1978   *Pastoral Care with Handicapped Persons.* Howard J. Clinebell, Jr. (ed.).
          Creative Pastoral Care and Counseling Series. Philadelphia: Fortress
          Press.
Cooper, B.
  1992   "The Disabled God," *Theology Today* 49 (2): 173-82.

Costas, O. E.
1989   *Christ Outside the Gate: Mission Beyond Christendom.* Maryknoll, N.Y.: Orbis Books.

Driedger, D.
1989   *The Last Civil Rights Movement: Disabled Peoples' International.* New York: St. Martin's Press.
Dworkin, A., and R. Dworkin (eds.)
1976   *The Minority Report.* New York: Praeger.

Eisenberg, M. G., C. Griggins, and R. J. Duval (eds.)
1982   *Disabled People as Second-Class Citizens.* New York: Springer.

Fiedler, L.
1978   *Freaks: Myths and Images of the Secret Self.* New York: Simon and Schuster.
1981   *Pity and Fear: Images of the Disabled in Literature and the Popular Arts.* United Nations: International Center for the Disabled.
Fine, M., and A. Asch (eds).
1988   *Women with Disabilities: Essays in Psychology, Culture and Politics.* Philadelphia: Temple University Press.
Finkelstein, V.
1980a   *Five Attitudes and Disabled People.* New York: World Rehabilitation Fund.
1980b   *Attitudes and Disabled People: Issues for Discussion.* New York: World Rehabilitation Fund.
Foucault, M.
1980   *Power/Knowledge: Selected Interviews and Other Writings 1972–1977.* New York: Pantheon Books.

Fourez, G.
1983   *Sacraments and Passages: Celebrating the Tensions of Modern Life.* Notre Dame: Ave Maria.

Frank, G.
1981   *Venus on Wheels: The Life History of a Congenital Amputee.* Ph.D. Dissertation, Department of Anthropology, University of California, Los Angeles.
1985   "'Becoming the Other': Empathy and Biographical Interpretation." *Biography* 8:189-210.
1988a   "On Embodiment: A Case Study of Congenital Limb Deficiency in American Culture." In M. Fine and A. Asch (eds.), *Women with Disabilities* (pp. 41-71). Philadelphia: Temple University Press.
1988b   "Beyond Stigma: Visibility and Self-Empowerment of Persons with Congenital Limb Deficiencies." *Journal of Social Issues* 44:95-115.
Freire, P.
1970   *Pedagogy for the Oppressed.* New York: Herder and Herder.
Funk, R.
1987   "Disability Rights: From Caste to Class in the Context of Civil Rights." In A. Gartner and T. Joe (eds.), *Images of the Disabled, Disabling Images* (pp. 7-30). New York: Praeger.

131

Geertz, C.
  1973   *The Interpretation of Cultures: Selected Essays.* New York: Basic Books.
Glaser, B. G., and A. L. Strauss
  1967   *The Discovery of Grounded Theory: Strategies for Qualitative Research.*
          Chicago: Aldine.
Gliedman, J., and W. Roth
  1980   *The Unexpected Minority: Handicapped Children in America.* New York:
          Harcourt Brace Jovanovich.
Goffman, E.
  1963   *Stigma: Notes on the Management of Spoiled Identity.* Englewood Cliffs:
          Prentice Hall.
  1982   *Interaction Ritual.* New York: Pantheon Books.
Govig, S.
  1985   "Children of a Lesser God." *Dialog* 24:246-47.
  1989   *Strong at the Broken Places: Persons with Disabilities and the Church.*
          Louisville: Westminster/John Knox Press.
Grant, J.
  1989   *White Women's Christ and Black Women's Jesus: Feminist Christology and
          Womanist Response.* Atlanta: Scholars Press.
Gussow, Z., and G. Tracy
  1968a   "Status, Ideology, and Adaptation to Stigmatized Illness: A Study of
          Leprosy." *Human Organization* 27:316-25.
  1968b   "The Role of Self-Help Clubs in Adaptation to Chronic Illness and
          Disability," *Social Science and Medicine* 10.
Gutiérrez, G.
  1988   *A Theology of Liberation.* 15th Anniversary Edition. Maryknoll, N.Y.:
          Orbis Books.

Hahn, H.
  1987   "Civil Rights for Disabled Americans: The Foundation of a Political
          Agenda." In A. Gartner and T. Joe (eds.), *Images of the Disabled,
          Disabling Images* (pp. 181-203). New York: Praeger.
  1988   "Politics of Physical Difference." *Journal of Social Issues* 44:39-47.
Halpern, S.
  1988   "Portrait of the Artist." Review of *Under the Eye of the Clock*, by
          Christopher Nolan. *New York Review of Books,* June 30, 3-4.
Harrison, B. W.
  1985   *Making the Connections: Essays in Feminist Social Ethics.* C. S. Robb (ed.).
          Boston: Beacon Press.
Heyward, C.
  1984   *Our Passion for Justice: Images of Power, Sexuality, and Liberation.* New
          York: Pilgrim Press.
Higgins, P. C.
  1980   "Societal Reaction and the Physically Disabled: Bring the Impairment
          Back In." *Symbolic Interaction* 3:139-56.
Hillyer, B.
  1993   *Feminism and Disability.* Norman, Okla.: University of Oklahoma Press.

Holmes, S. A.
1990   "The Disabled Find a Voice, and Make Sure It Is Heard." *New York Times,* March 18, E5.
1991   *New York Times,* September 30, A8.
hooks, bell.
1989   *Talking Back.* Boston: South End Press.

Johnson, M.
1990   "Accessing the Dream." *Spinal Column* 44:8-9.
Jones, M. L., and J. Hannah
1990   "Reflections on a New Decade." *Disability Rag* (January/February): 14-16.

Kleck, R.
1968   "Physical Stigma and Nonverbal Cues Emitted in Face-to-Face Interaction." *Human Relations* 21:19-28.
Kleck, R., H. Ono, and A. Hastorf
1966   "The Effects of Physical Deviance upon Face-to-Face Interaction." *Human Relations* 19:425-36.
Kriegel, L.
1987   "The Cripple in Literature." In A. Gartner and T. Joe (eds.), *Images of the Disabled, Disabling Images* (pp. 31-46). New York: Praeger.

Lane, N. J.
1993   "Healing Bodies and Victimization of Persons: Issues of Faith-Healing for Persons with Disabilities." *The Disability Rag Resource 14 (3): 11-13.*
Lerner, M. J.
1970   "The Desire for Justice and the Reaction to Victims." In J. Macauley and L. Berkowitz (eds.), *Altruism and Helping Behaviors.* New York: Academic Press.
Lischer, J., and L. Lischer
1985   "No Handicapped Ministers Need Apply." *Christian Century* 102:670-71.
Longmore, Paul K.
1985   "A Note on the Language and the Social Identity of Disabled People." *American Behavioral Scientist* 28:419-23.
Lorde, A.
1984   *Sister Outsider.* Trumansburg, N.Y.: Crossing Press.

Mairs, N.
1986   *Plaintext.* Tucson: University of Arizona.
1989   *Remembering the Bone House: An Erotics of Place and Space.* New York: Harper & Row, Publishers.
1990   *Carnal Acts.* New York: HarperCollins.
1993   *Ordinary Time: Cycles in Marriage, Faith and Renewal.* Boston: Beacon Press.
"Malnutrition Disables 100 Million," *One World,* 62:13.

133

Meeker, B. F., and P. A. Weitzel-O'Neill
 1977   "Sex Roles and Interpersonal Behavior in Task-Oriented Groups."
        American Sociological Review 42:91-105.
Meyerson, L.
 1988   "The Social Psychology of Physical Disability: 1948 and 1988." *Journal
        of Social Issues* 44:173-88.
Miles, M.
 1989   *Carnal Knowing: Female Nakedness and Religious Meaning in the Christian
        West.* Boston: Beacon Press.
Moltmann, J.
 1977   *The Church in the Power of the Spirit: A Contribution to Messianic
        Ecclesiology.* San Francisco: Harper & Row, Publishers.
Morrison, T.
 1973   *Sula.* New York: New American Library.
Mussen, P. H., and R. G. Barker
 1944   "Attitudes Toward Cripples." *Journal of Abnormal and Social Psychology*
        39:351-55.

Nagi, S. Z.
 1979   "The Concept and Measurement of Disability in Disability Policies
        and Government Programs." In E. D. Berkowitz (ed.), *Disability
        Policies and Government Programs* (pp. 1-15). New York: Praeger.
National Center for Health Statistics.
 1989   *Health, United States, 1989.* Hyattsville, Md.: U.S. Public Health
        Service. DHHS Pub. No. (PHS) 90-1232.
National Institute on Disability Rehabilitation Research.
 1989   *Chartbook on Disability in the United States.* An InfoUse Report.
        Washington, D.C.: U.S. Government Printing Office.

Oliver, M.
 1990   *The Politics of Disablement.* New York: St. Martin's Press.

O'Neill, D.
 1984   "Silent No More: The Disabled Move to the Front of the Bus."
        Progressive (December): 22-24.

Parsons, T.
 1951   *The Social System.* Glencoe, Ill.: Free Press.
 1964   *Social Structure and Personality.* New York: Free Press.
Percy, S.
 1989   *Disability, Civil Rights and Public Policy: The Politics of Implementation.*
        Tuscaloosa: University of Alabama Press.
Phillips, M.
 1988   "Disability and Ethnicity in Conflict: A Study of Transformation." In
        M. Fine and A. Asch (eds.), *Women with Disabilities* (pp. 195-214).
        Philadelphia: Temple University Press.

Ramshaw, E.
 1987   *Ritual and Pastoral Care.* Philadelphia: Fortress Press.

Rich, A.
1976   *Of Woman Born: Motherhood as Experience and Institution.* New York:
        W. W. Norton & Co.
Richardson, S. A., A. H. Hastorf, N. Goodman, and S. M. Dornbusch
1961   "Cultural Uniformity in Reaction to Physical Disabilities." *American
        Sociological Review* 26:241-47.
Ricoeur, P.
1967   *The Symbolism of Evil,* trans. Emerson Buchanan. Boston: Beacon
        Press.
1976   *Interpretation Theory: Discourse and the Surplus of Meaning.* Fort Worth:
        Texas Christian University Press.
Russell, L. M.
1993   *Church in the Round: Feminist Interpretation of the Church.* Louisville:
        Westminster/John Knox Press.

Safilios-Rothschild, C.
1970   *The Sociology and Social Psychology of Disability and Rehabilitation.* New
        York: Random House, 1970.
1981   "Disabled Persons Self-Definition and Their Implications for
        Rehabilitation." In G. Albrecht (ed.), *The Sociology of Physical Disability
        and Rehabilitation* (Pittsburgh: University of Pittsburgh Press, 1976),
        pp. 9-56.
Scarey, E.
1985   *The Body in Pain: The Making and Unmaking of the World.* New York:
        Oxford University Press.
Scheer, J., and N. Groce
1988   "Impairment as a Human Constant: Cross-Cultural and Historical
        Perspectives on Variation." *Journal of Social Issues* 44:23-38.
Schutz, A.
1962   "On Multiple Realities." *Collected Papers,* vol. 1. The Hague: Martinus
        Nijhoff.
Scotch, R.
1984   *From Good Will to Civil Rights: Transforming Federal Disability Policy.*
        Philadelphia: Temple University Press.
1988   "Disability as the Basis for a Social Movement: Advocacy and the
        Politics of Definition." *Journal of Social Issues* 44:159-72.
1989   "Politics and Policy in the History of the Disability Rights Movement,"
        Milbank Quarterly, 1989, 67, suppl. 2 (2): 380-400.
Shapiro, J. P.
1993   *No Pity: People with Disabilities Forging a New Civil Rights Movement.* New
        York: Times Books.
Silver, R., and C. Wortman.
1980   "Coping with Undesirable Life Events." In J. Gerber and M. Seligman
        (eds.), *Human Helplessness, Theory and Applications.* London:
        Academic Press.
Smith, D.
1987   *The Everyday World as Problematic.* Boston: Northeastern University
        Press.

Soelle, D.
   1974   *Political Theology.* Philadelphia: Fortress Press.

Thomas, D.
   1982   *The Experience of Handicap.* London: Methuen.
Tracy, D.
   1987   "Practical Theology in the situation of Global Pluralism." In L. S.
             Mudge and J. N. Poling (eds.), *Formation and Reflection* (pp. 139-54).
             Philadelphia: Fortress Press.
Tringo, J. L.
   1970   "The Hierarchy of Preference Toward Disability Groups." *Journal of
             Special Education* 4:295-306.
Turner, B. S.
   1984   *The Body and Society: Explorations in Social Theory.* Oxford: Basil
             Blackwell.
Tyor, P. L., and L. V. Bell
   1984   *Caring for the Retarded in America: A History.* Westport, Conn.:
             Greenwood Press.

Welch, S.
   1985   *Communities of Resistance and Solidarity: A Feminist Theology of Liberation.*
             Maryknoll, N.Y.: Orbis Books.
   1990   *A Feminist Ethic of Risk.* Minneapolis: Fortress Press.
Wendell, S.
   1989   "Toward a Feminist Theory of Disability," *Hypatia* 4 (2): 104-24.
Wertlieb, E.
   1985   "Minority Group Status of the Disabled." *Human Relations* 38:1047-63.
Wirth, L.
   1970   "The Problem of Minority Groups." In M. Kurokawa (ed.), *Minority
             Responses: Comparative Views of Reactions to Subordination* (pp. 34-42).
             New York: Random House.

Young, I. M.
   1990   *Justice and the Politics of Difference.* Princeton University Press.

Zola, I.
   1982*a*   *Missing Pieces: A Chronicle of Living with Disability.* Philadelphia:
             Temple University Press.
   1982*b*   (ed.) *Ordinary Lives: Voices of Disability & Disease.* Cambridge:
             Applewood Books.
   1982*c*   "Social and Cultural Disincentives to Independent Living," *Archives
             of Physical Medicine and Rehabilitation,* vol. 63.

CPSIA information can be obtained at www.ICGtesting.com
Printed in the USA
LVOW132248100113

315237LV00002B/24/P